ARCHERY: THINK AND SHOOT LIKE A CHAMPION

TERRY WUNDERLE

ARCHERY: THINK AND SHOOT LIKE A CHAMPION

WUNDERLE ARCHERY
www.wunderlearchery.com

ISBN: 978-0-615-83489-4

Preface

Archery: Think and Shoot Like a Champion is a composite and blend of hundreds of articles that have been published over the past 30 years. Designed as an educational and instructional manual, this book teaches 3-D, target, and field archers, as well as hunters, how to overcome the mental and physical obstacles encountered when striving to become champions in their sport. Basic concepts are reinforced throughout the text so that articles may be read in order or used selectively as references. Author Terry Wunderle, better known as "The Archery Shot Doctor," is one of the most successful professional archery coaches in the world. He has coached students to over 350 national and world titles, while watching them set over 450 national and world records. Terry conducts archery schools across the United States, helping students to overcome problems and achieve their goals. By sharing his methods and concepts in this book, he teaches archers how to experience greater success.

Dedication

Archery: Think and Shoot Like a Champion is dedicated to my parents, Steven Price and Ellen Wunderle, and my three children, Dawn Stultz, Vic Wunderle, and Sally Seipp. My parents encouraged my interest in archery when they gave me my first commercial bow at age nine. This gesture was partially motivated by their desire to protect the trees in our area, as I had been removing limbs to create bows and arrows. When I started helping my own children on their way to becoming world-class archers, I found I had to develop coaching techniques that would foster their success. I thank my family for being willing test subjects and an inspiration.

Acknowledgement

This book would never have been written if it were not for the motivation and countless hours of effort by my wife, Jeanne. Thank you for your encouragement and dedication.

To my editor, Melissa Karlin, thank you for your organizational expertise, patience with editing, and making *Archery: Think and Shoot Like a Champion* become a reality.

John and Gaye Maxson, your assistance with cover and photo layout and professional expertise with the printing process have been greatly appreciated.

To my brother, Steve Wunderle, thank you for sharing your knowledge as an outdoor writer and published author of numerous books.

I am grateful that God has brought so many fine archers into my life and allowed me to coach them.

Table of Contents

Chapter 1. The Sport of Archery

What Makes a Great Archer?

"What makes a great archer and how do I become one of them?" is a question pondered by most people who launch an arrow. As the world's highest-achieving archers continue to reach new levels of performance, two common characteristics become evident: these elite athletes have a trouble-free form and trouble-free thinking.

Trouble-free form is one that uses the correct muscles to execute a rhythmic shot in exactly the same manner every time. There are many small variations of this form. An archer can make slight deviations of a great form to modify it to fit his or her comfort zone since all archers do not conform to one mold. However, there are a few basic concepts of the perfect form that are not changed by any of the best archers. The main factor is that they all pull the bow apart as they release the arrow; this is a must. Another aspect is almost all great archers shoot each arrow with the same rhythm so that nearly every shot is within 1 second of the same time frame. By maintaining consistent rhythm, an archer will be more prone to duplicate the pressure needed to produce the shot. The only way this can be accomplished is by believing in your form and trusting the shot execution, rather than trusting the sight picture and being hesitant with the release. A hesitant shot breaks down the consistent pressure needed to shoot good form. The sight pin always has some movement, but forward pressure with the bow arm reduces the movement to a minimum. The next time you observe excessive movement in the sight, add about 1 pound of extra forward pressure. The sight movement will then be minimized.

What is trouble-free thinking? I would best describe it as a positive and calm thought process. It does not dwell on the results of the last arrow shot or the outcome of the arrow in your bow. It is not centered on results such as wins or scores. Different thoughts go through the minds of each archer, but the common factors are that they are positive and calming. The archers whom I coach are thinking optimistically about their ability to use perfect form. They do this with every shot in practice as well as with every shot in a tournament. The only thing archers can actually control is their ability to execute a perfect shot. You cannot control what's on the scorecards, so why waste time dwelling on it? Practice helps you to perfect the ability to duplicate your shot, which gives you the confidence to trust and shoot that same shot under tournament conditions.

There are more excellent archers today than there were 10 years ago. The reason for this is because the knowledge of what it takes to become great has been shared by many outstanding athletes and coaches. The learning curve has been reduced for people entering the sport, which is why young people can shoot competitively with experienced archers. What the veterans learned in 20 years, a beginner can accomplish in 2 years with the proper instruction. The most important piece of advice that I would give any archer is to believe in your ability to execute a shot with perfect form; then trust yourself and shoot that shot.

Lighten Up and Have Fun

When our son Vic was 14 years old, he and I were fascinated as we watched a 5-year-old shooting his bow. If an arrow hit the target, the young archer would explode with excitement, laughing and yelling ecstatically. It was a humorous scene to watch. On the way home, Vic remarked, "That's what archery should be about. The little boy was having fun." He went on to explain that he was feeling the effects of burnout and he wasn't enjoying himself as much. By shooting a compound bow and release, he felt that he should never miss the X ring. When he did, negative feelings crept in, but there was no positive reward for the perfect shots because that was what he expected.

Soon afterwards, our good friend Gail Martin sent him an Olympic-style bow and Vic put his compound equipment into retirement. Because of the challenge and enjoyment, Vic has stayed with the recurve bow, which has led him down a path to multiple national and world titles, and 2 Olympic medals. The main reason for Vic's burnout in his youth, I blame on his over-zealous father and coach who pushed for excellence. One of the best pieces of advice that I can share with any archer is that a parent should never coach his spouse or his children. It usually puts stress on their relationship.

How many times have we observed an archer who rarely missed a tournament for years and then totally disappeared from the sport? The answer is "too often"; so why did they quit? Shooter burnout! Vic best described this dilemma when he said, "I'm not having fun anymore."

The main cause for burnout is the continuous pressure put on the archer by the parent, coach or most often, himself or herself. Putting pressure on yourself and learning how to handle it is necessary to build a champion. What is typically overlooked, however, is that there have to be breaks from the pressure; it should not be a constant thing. Too often we forget the most important reason why we are shooting, which is for enjoyment. Very few of us make a living as a professional archer, but even the professional ones have to enjoy archery or they, too, become a casualty of burnout.

Years ago I went to my first Indoor National Target Championship and I could not believe the pressure and tension that radiated from the participants. On the second day, I walked down to watch the professional competitors. There was one guy laughing and joking with everyone. I asked a fellow archer, “Does that guy know he is shooting in the championship?”

He replied, “Yes, I think he is in first. That’s Frank Pearson.” Frank’s love and enjoyment of the sport helped keep him a top-level shooter for several decades.

Most archers want to become a champion. I once read a piece written by Julie Ford in an Illinois Archery Association Newsletter and it helped me understand what really makes a winner. She wrote of two different champion archers who faced adversity, ignored it, and shot the tournament. One athlete had her bow stolen moments before the event, so she borrowed one from another participant and still competed. The other archer was inadvertently told the wrong starting time for the Indoor State Championship. She showed up late and missed shooting her first ten arrows. Instead of giving up, she laughed and went on to complete a perfect score on the remaining targets. Neither archer went home with a trophy, but both were truly winners because they loved and enjoyed our great sport. Each of us should ask ourselves, “Would I have gone ahead and shot the tournament?” If the answer is “no,” I would say you probably show one of the symptoms of burnout.

Another common symptom is when archery becomes just another job and you do not anxiously look forward to the next competition. Perhaps your attitude has become negative and you continually complain about your shooting, equipment or scores. Maybe you do not look forward to practice because you view it as work. If this should happen to be the case, then let us look at some of the ways to avoid the pitfalls of burnout.

The best cure is an attitude adjustment. Why are you shooting? I hope you will answer, "Because I enjoy it." Remember, that is why you got started. You should look forward to practice and have fun doing it; if not, add zest and some meaning to your practice sessions. Set a goal for each workout, such as achieving a certain score on a "dot target" or maybe executing perfect form while shooting blank bale. I personally love practice because it is a time to work with my equipment and get it tuned up like a fine-running race car.

Use practice time to experiment with various arrows, points or vanes; adjust the tiller settings to test arrow groups; or experiment with different stabilizers. There are all kinds of goals that you can create to give practice meaning; and just as importantly, they will make you concentrate in order to achieve them. Doing the same old thing in practice every time will produce boredom, and boredom fosters burnout.

We have a lot of fun on our range when we become creative with our practice routines. One favorite game is tick-tack-toe with balloons representing the squares. This is enjoyable for any age of archers and the distance at which the balloons are shot can vary according to the ability of the shooters. Another exercise is to put up a multicolored bullseye target and then divide the target in half by making a vertical line across the face. One archer shoots at the left half and the other shoots at the right, releasing a total of 5 arrows and trying to place one in each color. If there are 2 or more in one color, only 1 counts. At the end of the round, the points are totaled to determine the winner. A third game is what we call "Five Shot Walk Back." We use a bullseye target and take one shot at each distance of 20 through 60 yards at 10-yard intervals. When the round ends, the score is tallied to establish the winner.

Archery is one of the most enjoyable sports available to all people, and age or gender is not a determining factor as to how well you can perform. If you want to avoid the symptoms of burnout, you might want to think of the advice my daughter Sally gave me when she insisted, "Lighten up, Dad. You have to have fun."

Why Shoot Tournaments?

Years ago, some friends talked me into going to a three-dimensional (3-D) tournament and since then, there was no turning back. Over the years, I have competed with hundreds of interesting, knowledgeable people. Socializing and meeting other participants is an important aspect of archery, so I try to shoot with someone new at each event. This has led to many new friendships and provided valuable insights about the sport.

While the reasons people enter these tournaments vary, the one common thread is the challenge. Universally, I have found the hardest fought competition is that between the shooter and himself or herself. Three-dimensional archery presents unique and interesting challenges, as well as rewards to its enthusiasts.

3-D Targets Evolved from Paper

Three-dimensional target tournaments can trace their

origins to hunters using paper pictures to practice simulated shots at animals. As time went by, technology yielded new materials suitable for archery targets. Innovative bow hunters began cutting out two-dimensional (2-D) animal silhouettes. These hunters had so much fun shooting the 2-D animal forms that clubs began sponsoring tournaments. The sport finally progressed to the use of the 3-D targets, which are presently utilized in national and world competitions.

Innovations in archery equipment changed rapidly when the archery industry realized that hunters and 3-D archers out-numbered target shooters. Speed, in addition to accuracy, became the name of the game, and bows and arrows were designed to meet this new demand. Previously, arrow speeds of 300 feet or more per second had been rare; now they have become commonplace.

Three Categories of Shooters

Most 3-D archers fall into one of three categories: the bow hunters, the "fun shooters," and the serious competitors. Mention a 3-D tournament and people often think of the dedicated 3-D competitor. This is not what the sport is all about; the serious competitor is in the minority, while most archers at the local level tournaments consist of hunters and those who are there just to have a good time. The local club's challenge is to accommodate all three of these groups. Because of the larger number of bow hunters and "fun shooters," most clubs set their targets closer to the participant, usually an average of 20–35 yards. Regional and national competitions stretch the shooting distances out to challenge the serious competitors.

Bow Hunters

There is no question that one benefit of these tournaments has been to raise the efficiency of the average deer hunter. Through 3-D competitions, bow hunters have learned the importance of accurately judging yardage and how to concentrate on hitting a particular spot. As a bow hunter tries to catch the 10 ring, he or she learns to deal with pressure and to stay focused. This type of training makes a shot much easier when a real buck comes within range during deer season. Every hunter benefits from participating in several 3-D tournaments a year. In keeping with the original purpose, one of the best and most important goals accomplished by the 3-D shoots is the help they give to the deer hunter.

“Fun Shooters”

The “fun shooters” are mainly recreational archers and children. These are often the people who get the most enjoyment from the sport. What a reward it is to watch a youngster release an arrow at a target and react with excitement when he or she hits the mark. Participants of all ages can have a great time being together and shooting their bows, which is what the sport is all about. Too often archers, including me, let scores interfere with having fun.

Serious Competitors

The last group of archers is the serious competitor. Those who fall in this group work hard at being the best in their class, whether it is on a local, state, or national level. They are dedicated to the sport and work hard at performing to the best of their capabilities. They are also good for archery because they display the degree of efficiency one can acquire with a bow and give others the motivation to improve.

No matter which category of 3-D archery you fall into, the most important thing is to enjoy it as a sport. Most archers are among the nicest people you will ever meet. I encourage others to shoot with different participants and to take the time to visit with those attending the tournaments. If you need help or have questions, go up to a fellow archer and speak with him or her. This is probably how that person learned to shoot the bow.

A sincere thank you goes to all of the clubs that host the competitions and help produce better sportsmen. As archers benefit from the sport, it is important that each one tries to give something back. One of the greatest aspects of archery is that people of all ages can compete on an equal basis. I would like to suggest that each of you introduce a young person to the sport. Children are our future archers. If a youngster wants to learn how to shoot, then he or she is old enough to start. Each of my 3 children came to me and asked to participate when they were five or six years old. The main factor is that the child must want to learn.

How Family and Friends Help You

On the second day of competition at an indoor national championship, one of my students found himself in second place with only two "X's" out of first. Just before the starting whistle, I encouraged him to not be concerned with the score or winning and to just shoot good form. I also told him to not worry about the boy in first because I doubted that he would even place. When the tournament ended, my student discovered he had a solid victory. He came to me and asked, "How did you know the guy in first wouldn't even place?" I then explained that the young man was very nervous and his father was escalating the degree of pressure by constantly reminding him that he needed to shoot “X’s” to win.

Friends and relatives can unknowingly be your worst enemies at a tournament. All archers self-inflict some degree of pressure on themselves because they would like to shoot a good score or have a winning performance. When the hopes, encouragement, and expectations of others are included, the pressure can become unmanageable. In certain sports, such as football and soccer, being “fired up” is usually to the athlete’s advantage because this extra nervousness will increase the energy output. However, sports like archery and golf require that the competitor stay calm and relaxed. Excessive tension will produce anxiety and tighten muscles that are needed to produce a smooth, rhythmic shot.

You have to understand that friends or family members are nervous and anxious about your performance. They want to help and support you in hopes that you will be successful. Unfortunately, their kindhearted intentions can be detrimental. Their focus on the score and winning can distract you and increase the tension.

When you think you are cheering someone on, are you actually creating unnecessary stress? My daughter Sally and I had a good relationship when it came to tournaments. If she had problems with her form, I would help her. Other than that, my role was to stay calm and keep the atmosphere lighthearted and fun. Several times at competitions, she asked me to leave and watch from a distance. She knew that there was too much stress and concern in my face and body language. She did not need that. I would tell her, “I love you … and enjoy the tournament,” as I walked away.

As an archer, are those close to you harming your performance? If so, you need to have a serious conversation with them. Describe to them what kind of tournament relationship would be the most beneficial for you. When they are saying and doing things that bother you, address these issues. Trying to change the situation can be like trying to remove a bad stain from a carpet. You have to keep working at it. During a competition, if the comments of others are counterproductive, remind them of the role that you wish for them to assume.

I truly believe that anyone who can shoot good scores in practice can produce them in tournament play. Skillful practice shots are produced because the archer is relaxed and attentive. The key to success is to develop a similar mental program for competition. Ask your family and friends to work with you to keep your performance calm and focused.

Chapter 2. Shoot Form

Develop a Consistent Form

Years ago, I talked Jamie Van Natta into changing from a finger shooter to a release shooter. This young lady was very dedicated to becoming a champion. For two months, she practiced with a blank bale and never shot an arrow at a target. This time was used to develop her concentration skills and a strong, consistent form. As the years passed, Jamie rose to the top of her sport and became recognized as one of the world's elite archers.

Practice is the main foundation that an athlete has to build upon in order to be successful. Quality practice gives you stamina, muscle memory, confidence, and enhanced concentration level. I prefer to separate practice into two categories: form practice and performance practice. In order to be a successful archer, you must be able to shoot the shot with the same, precise form every time. This means using the same rhythm, the same amount of back tension, and the same explosive force. The bow arm and the release hand should complete the shot in the identical position at the conclusion of each shot. The best way to achieve this is to start with blank bale shooting. Feel the muscles used in the execution of the shot; then, concentrate on applying the same degree of muscle tension with each practice shot.

If you are starting a new season and have not practiced for an extended period of time, you should spend a week or longer perfecting your form and developing muscle memory with blank bale shooting. Once you feel positive about your form, take it to the next level by placing a five-spot target at 10 yards and shoot at it. Aiming is part of the shot process and needs to be phased into the program.

Shooting the target at 10 yards requires you to aim but does not put too much emphasis on the process. This will allow you to focus more on perfect shot execution. After a week of practicing in this manner, try placing the target at 20 yards. If you find that you are not shooting the same shot at the 20-yard target, begin alternating every other shot using the blank bale, but do not be concerned where the arrow hits. Try to get the blank bale form to identically mirror that of the target shot. Once the two match, you will have a form that should put you on the road to success. I cannot stress enough that being able to shoot the same, identical shot is one of the most important factors necessary to be a skilled archer.

When you have refined your form, you should have also developed stamina and muscle memory. Now, work on your confidence and concentration. It makes no difference whether you are a 3-D, field, FITA, or target archer, because all of these require the same basic foundation in order to be successful. You must execute the shot in an identical manner every time. Mount a five-spot target at 20 yards again and now shoot for points. Because score is part of the game, you must learn to deal with it. This is the way you develop your concentration level. Focus and execute every shot the same, but do not let your mind float off into "Lala Land." As your groups tighten and your scores rise, so will your confidence. You are proving to yourself that you are capable of replicating every shot.

There are many components to a winning archery program, but one of the most important elements is a strong foundation upon which to build. Begin your season by spending several weeks with the goal of developing consistent form. The perfect shot is a feeling, and you will know it is a perfect shot when it is released. Concentrate and try to duplicate this feeling.

Avoid Target Panic

As one of my students stood on the practice range and warmed up for the start of a big tournament, I noticed a premature movement in his bow arm just before the shot was released. Approaching him, I firmly suggested, "Quit aiming and get your mind where it belongs." He knew exactly what I meant.

At one time or another, most archers are hampered by the effects of target panic. I like to describe the condition as the involuntary reaction to a "fear of missing." It usually happens when too many negative thoughts are going through the archer's mind as the shot is being executed. The archer is uncomfortable with the situation and worried about missing, which then results in a panic attack.

I truly believe the main cause of target panic is over-aiming. Far too much emphasis is placed on "Aim! Aim! Aim!" When this is the primary focus, the brain is giving the archer a green light "yes" signal if the pin is on the mark and a red light "no" signal when it is not. During a typical shot sequence, the subconscious and/or conscious mind is sending these opposing commands to the voluntary muscles used in the shot process. Consequently, the shot execution starts and stops until the arrow is finally released. Such conflict heightens the archer's level of tension. Since the emphasis is on aiming, the mixed signals end up giving the shooter target panic.

Then what is the best way to avoid or overcome target panic? For successful shot execution, the archer should shoot from the conscious mind and keep the focus where it belongs – on form. Most shots are missed because of a breakdown in form, rather than the failure to place the pin perfectly on the target. When muscles are tightened in order to center the pin precisely on the mark, one is actually causing additional sight movement and increasing the "yes-no" effect. A relaxed form that allows the pin to float will have far less movement and will let the bow arm react the same way each time the arrow is released.

To avoid target panic, take charge of your thought process. Concentrate on producing each shot with perfect form, which is something you can control. Develop a positive mental image and greater confidence as you produce the shot sequence from your conscious mind. By focusing entirely on shooting with your best form, your mind will not be giving you the conflicting "yes-no" signals that create target panic.

If you are a finger shooter, make sure you have a consistent, clean release. For those using a mechanical release, I highly recommend one with back tension. There is no trigger to intensify the "yes-no" effect. All you need to do is allow the pin to float on the target and pull with your back muscles until the release goes off. With back tension, you are forced to shoot good form if it is set off properly. Many of the archers whom I coach practice with a back tension release, but shoot a trigger release at the tournaments. Training in this manner helps them develop correct form and prevents them from experiencing target panic. Because target panic is a mental problem, eliminate it with your mind and *focus on form*.

Own Your Shot

Some years ago, one of my top archers was shooting an indoor target championship and doing exceptionally well. Another coach asked me, "Why do you let him shoot with his feet like that?" (He was referring to the very closed stance of Braden Gellenthien.)

I replied, "It was the only way that we could get him to drive his front end through the shot."

"It just doesn't look right," he said.

I pointed out, "It has worked for him. He is only 17 years old and has set twenty-five world records."

At the time, Braden's style was a little different from what might have been expected as perfect archery form. I would not have recommended for anyone to copy it, but Braden owned his shot and was able to duplicate it every time. It is unusual to see any two people with identical form, although the form of most good archers is very similar. A common denominator is the ability to drive the bow arm through the shot. You have to find the variation of good form with which you are comfortable and then practice until every shot can be exactly duplicated. That is when you "own your shot."

If you have a variation in your form that is not the same with every execution, then I would suggest you make a change. It is best to make these alterations at the beginning of the season and then stay with them. Do not go through a season constantly making changes in your form. Most variations can be duplicated under calm practice conditions, but can they be reproduced during the intensity of a big tournament? The best example of this is an archer who shoots what I call a "soft shot," where the execution has a weak explosion when the arrow is released. Yes, it can usually be duplicated in practice, but very few archers can replicate it under pressure conditions. Why? When tournament tension builds, they can become a little too pumped and shoot too strong a shot, producing a high-hitting arrow. In many cases, the opposite happens when the archer tries to over-aim the shot. The result is a weaker explosion, shooting a low arrow.

So what is the answer? If you look at the top-winning archers, nearly all of them have a strong explosive shot. I want my shooters to pull the bow apart to release the arrow. This is the case for both finger shooters and release shooters. A strong shot is much easier to duplicate, especially under high pressure situations. If a strong shot becomes a little weaker, the odds are very good that it will still hit the mark. If a weak shot becomes weaker, the wheels of the bow will no longer be solid against the wall. The arrow will begin to creep forward and a bad shot is inevitable.

To be a skillful archer, you not only need to shoot a strong shot, you must maintain a consistent rhythm. As previously noted, top scoring archers shoot nearly every shot within one second of the same time frame, while allowing the pin to settle in on the mark and then pulling the bow apart to release the arrow. In practice and in competition, strive to trust your own shot and do not "yes-no" the process. Though there will always be some pin movement, the strong forward pressure with the bow arm will minimize that movement. When you commit to the execution, do just that and shoot. As long as you drive the bow arm at the mark, it will be a good shot.

Quit Aiming!

When he was younger, Braden Gellenthien was shooting the first end of 70 meters at the beginning of the Junior World Trials. As he finished his six arrows, he came off the line and shook his head in disgust, even though he had made a perfect score of 60. Then he approached me and said, "I know. I'm aiming too much and it will stop."

When a competition heats up and the scores are close, archers tend to place more pressure on themselves, often trying to be too precise with the shot placement. By doing this, they add several seconds to their normal shooting rhythm and cause a breakdown in their form. Usually, the added time results in a weaker follow-through with the bow arm, producing a low or low-right shot (low-left shot for left-handers). When over-aiming happens, the bow arm loses forward pressure and more sight movement occurs. A weak shot is likely to follow.

The problem of over-aiming starts when one's thinking process is centered on the score or winning. Such pressure often begins days before a tournament and intensifies after the competition gets underway. Focusing on scores and first place is an excellent blueprint for a poor performance. Then where should you direct your attention? Picture yourself shooting your best possible form. This process will build a positive image, help you relax, and produce a more excellent shot.

Many archers put their confidence in the sight picture, not their form. When they get nervous and see sight movement, their game begins to deteriorate. Very few archers are steady enough to "lock on" to the X ring and have the pin stay there. They keep waiting for the shot, wanting the pin to hold on the mark. This can also add several seconds to their normal shooting rhythm, which allows the back pressure to decrease and sets the stage for an ineffective shot.

How can you remedy the problem? Trust your form, not your sight. If you tighten muscles in an attempt to guide the sight pin, the effect of this tension will be reflected in the shot execution. Concentrate and make sure you produce a shot with your best form. If the form is good, the result will be much better than if you had continued aiming.

To prove this concept to yourself so you will trust your form, place a 40-centimeter target at forty yards and shoot twenty arrows for score. Now, repeat the process, but let the pin float as you shoot a rhythmic shot and concentrate on form. The scores should confirm where to place your trust. The next time you find yourself in a pressure situation, you should have the skills to make a good shot. Instead of worrying about erratic pin movement, focus on perfect shot execution. Having confidence and trust in your form will help you perform like a champion.

Relaxed Aiming

On one occasion, I was shooting a 3-D course with a couple of friends and we were faced with a very challenging shot. The target was a 42-yard black bear nestled in dark brush. Due to the sunlight in our faces, it was very difficult to see the bear, let alone make out the vitals. Once we drew the bow and looked through the peep, it nearly disappeared. I shot first and heard the friendly sound of foam. The next two archers were not as fortunate.

When we arrived at the target, I discovered that I had scored a solid 10. One of the archers asked, “How did you do that? I couldn’t even see the target when I looked through my peep.”

My reply was, “I started aiming before I drew my bow and you started after you looked through the peep. Once you look through the peep some visibility was lost because less reflected light was entering your eye.”

The aiming finishes after addressing the target. You should pick out the exact spot that you want your arrow to hit. Your primary vision should remain on that spot until after the arrow has made contact. After selecting your aiming point, place your pin on it and then draw your bow. Keep your primary vision on that point and your secondary vision on the pin. The pin will automatically move to the desired aiming point. If you cannot place your pin on the target and draw the bow, I would guess that you are pulling more pounds than you can handle.

Once you are at full draw and looking through the peep, you must relax all muscles except those needed to execute the shot. If the unnecessary muscles remain tightened, you will see jerky pin movement. Place a pencil in your bow hand and extend it to arm's length. Then, tighten all the muscles in that arm and aim the pencil at an object in the distance. You should observe jerky pin movement; and the longer that you hold it, the worse it gets. Now, try it again but relax all muscles except those needed to hold and aim the pencil. You should observe less movement and the movement that is present should be a slow floating motion. The top archers have learned or been taught to relax certain muscles that were required to draw the bow and then to use other muscles to execute the back pressure. This presents them with a sight picture with minimal pin movement.

When you reach a relaxed full draw and start the back pressure part of the shot execution, nearly all of the sight movement will disappear. If you are holding too many pounds or you have held the bow for too long of a period, your body and mind will say, "Hurry up and get the shot off!" At this point, one of two things can happen. You rush the shot execution and have questionable results or you let down and start over. The choice is very obvious.

It is very important that an archer remains relaxed during the final stages of the shot in order to minimize pin movement. If the best that you can do is to allow the pin to float in a small circle, then that is the type of shot you will have to take. Do not tighten unnecessary muscles to try to reduce the pin movement. These extra tight muscles will cause unwanted bow movement as the arrow leaves. The addition of tightened muscles will affect the reaction of the bow and the impact point of the arrow. Strength is not a determining factor in aiming. Only shoot the draw weight that you can aim comfortably. Being in good physical condition with good muscle tone is very helpful in reducing pin movement.

The last stage of aiming is the moment during and after the arrow leaves the bow. The primary vision of the archer must remain on the target and the head should not move. Too many people raise their heads to watch the arrow. When this happens, you will also move the bow arm and cause a bad shot. If you continue to focus on the 10 ring, the odds are much greater that your arrow will appear in it. The main trick to aiming is to relax and minimize pin movement. Hold the pin as close to the desired impact point as possible and execute a shot with consistent form.

Five Ways to Confirm Your Equipment Fits

For an archer to shoot consistently, he or she must remain comfortable and relaxed during the shot process. To accomplish this, the equipment needs to fit and be as satisfying as that old pair of shoes that should have been thrown away several years ago. Draw length, draw weight, grip, peep, and mass bow weight and balance are five things which can be examined in order to provide that comfortable fit when shooting.

Draw Length

The correct draw length is a critical issue. It is very difficult to have consistent form with a draw length that is too long. While standing at full draw with adequate back pressure, the bow shoulder should remain in a down position, as it is when standing with a relaxed posture. If the archer discovers that the shoulder has to come up in order to maintain forward pressure, the draw length is too long. Such a situation makes it difficult to maintain consistent back pressure, resulting in a breakdown of correct form. With proper draw length, the bow arm will either be locked out at the elbow or slightly bent. Either position should feel comfortable and solid when executing the shot.

Draw Weight

Draw weight is another critical issue that can cause a breakdown in form. There are several ways to confirm if draw weight is too high. By using the correct draw weight, the archer should be able to put the pin on the target and draw the bow. If the bow has to be pointed up or down in order to get enough leverage to draw, too many pounds are being pulled. Another way to check the weight is to see what happens when three or four seconds are added to the normal shot routine. Does the bow arm begin to tremble? Is the shot being rushed in order to avoid the increase in sight movement? These are indications of too much draw weight. Reduce the draw weight by three or four pounds and note if the arrow group tightens. Archers want speed. Sometimes 3-D archers are so obsessed with speed that they shoot too great a draw weight. Perhaps lowering the pounds and working on distance estimation would achieve more effective results. Remember, slow hits score higher than fast misses.

Grip

The grip on the bow can produce inconsistency in shooting form. The bow hand must be seated exactly the same on every shot. This can be difficult if the grip is too large or too rounded and the hand slides on it when at full draw. Wooden and plastic grips can be altered to fit the hand. Another option is to purchase a custom-made grip or to remove the grip and shoot off the riser.

Peep

The peep must be comfortable for shooting. When standing relaxed with the head over the bow shoulder, the head should not have to be moved from that position in order to look through the peep to shoot. Tilting the head up or down to see through the peep causes other muscles to tighten, which can produce tension in the shot process.

Mass Bow Weight and Balance

The mass bow weight and balance of the bow are touchy items. When balanced, the bow should roll forward as the arrow is released. This can be achieved by adding weight to the front of the stabilizer. An archer does not want the overall mass weight of the bow and accessories to be so heavy that it is difficult to hold when shooting. However, you do want the total mass weight to be as high as you can comfortably control. With the heavier weight, there is less sight movement. Shoot arrow groups using different weights and balances to determine the best combination for success.

When coaching an archer, one of the first things I determine is whether the equipment fits. With minor adjustments in the equipment, I often have seen the groups tighten instantly. Take the time to try different variations in the bow setup. The more comfortable the archer becomes with the equipment, the more relaxed and smooth the shot execution will be. The result is tighter arrow groups and a better performance.

Slow Hits Beat Fast Misses

I was watching a young archer on the practice range as he prepared for the tournament. He soon noticed me and we struck up a conversation.

"I really love my new bow," he remarked. "It shoots 315 feet per second, but I'm not scoring well. What am I doing wrong?"

When I asked him how many pounds of peak weight he was pulling, he responded that his bow was set at 75 pounds. Frankly, this was way too much weight for him, and I suggested that he drop his peak weight eight or ten pounds. He did, and shot a good, tight group.

Some archers think that drawing high poundage is a macho thing to do. Others have an obsession about high-speed arrows being a "cure all" for distance judging errors. In order to achieve these blazing speeds, they crank up the peak weight about as high as their strength will allow them to pull. Now, it may be true that they can pull back 65 or 70 pounds; but this leads to the real question, "How much can they hold steady while they are aiming?" At 65% let-off, some of these shooters are trying to aim while holding too many pounds.

If you are at full draw, your sight pin is bobbing around like a Mexican jumping bean, and you can't get it to hold steady on the target, this is a good indication that your body is saying “no” to the amount of weight you are trying to hold. If you feel you must hurry up and shoot the arrow or you will become unsteady, then your holding weight is too high.

In order to execute a shot with perfect form, the muscles in your body must stay relaxed. Excess draw weight will cause them to tighten and will result in inconsistent shot execution. Another problem with overextending the amount of weight you are trying to shoot is loss of back tension. Your back muscles have the ability to hold a certain amount of weight. You simply will not be able to maintain good tension of these back muscles if you try to hold too much weight without first developing more strength in those muscles. Without consistent, uniform back pressure of the release arm, the bow arm will collapse. When the bow arm moves, it is impossible to shoot a good group. Lack of back pressure, followed by moving the bow arm too quickly, is the most common accuracy problem archers typically face. An archer must have the ability to shoot each shot with consistent form in order to shoot tight groups. If the archer cannot handle the bow’s holding weight, good form and accuracy are impossible.

Here is a simple test to determine how much weight you should be shooting. First, shoot a group of arrows. Now, let the bow off by five pounds and shoot another group of arrows. Compare the two groups. The results should give you the answer.

A 3-D course is a mixture of close, medium, and long range targets. While it is true that faster arrow speed permits a greater margin of error in judging distance for the longer shots, it does very little for the closer targets. The price of higher speed achieved through higher draw weight is usually poorer form and fewer points. The higher speed may enable you to hit a few "lucky" 10's, but the few extra points you pick up this way are more than offset by the points you will more than likely lose because of poor form.

Shoot From Your Center of Gravity

We were shooting a 3-D course laid out on particularly rough terrain with many uphill, downhill, and side hill shots. It had been a challenging morning. As I was walking off the course, another archer stopped me. "Why am I missing to the right and to the left of the slopes?" he asked in frustration. "I have had my bow on a sight leveler, and I know that my bubble is correct."

We went to the practice range, part of which was also on a hillside. I watched him shoot a few arrows, and then stopped him. "Your bow is just fine," I suggested. "The problem is we need to put a level on you!" It is absolutely imperative that your head and shoulders are directly over your center of gravity for every shot that you make. When shooting on uneven surfaces, most archers have the tendency to overcorrect the center of balance to the point that they are leaning toward the hill. It is similar to what a person does when he or she is on a roof and looks over the edge. The individual actually leans back towards the roof in order to feel safer.

On a sloping hillside, the archer leans too far towards the hill because he or she feels more secure. A good example of this is a hillside shot where you are forced to stand in such a way that your toes are higher than your heels. You don't want to fall over backwards, so you lean into the hill, more than what is necessary, and you overcompensate. By doing this, both your bow and your release arm go more inward toward the center of the chest.

This action results in shooting a shot with less back pressure and a weak follow-through. A weak shot will usually produce a shot where the arrow hits to the right of the aiming point (or to the left for left-handers).

The exact opposite scenario occurs when you stand on a hill in such a way that your heels are higher than your toes. In this case, you will find yourself leaning backwards into the hill, with your head and shoulders ending up on the backside of your center of gravity. This usually produces a stronger shot because the shoulder blades come together with more force. Consequently, it will probably produce an arrow that impacts to the left side of the target (or the right side for left-handers).

How can you keep from overcorrecting on these shots? First, you must align your body before drawing back the bow. Stand up straight with your shoulders perpendicular to the target (if that is your usual shoulder alignment) and be sure that you are perfectly balanced. If you feel too much pressure on your toes or heels, it is an indication that you are probably leaning. When you are balanced, someone could hypothetically put a level along your spine and head and it would indicate that you are perpendicular to the ground. Once you are balanced, raise your bow and complete the shot without changing the center of gravity.

When shooting uphill or downhill targets, the balanced shooting position becomes more difficult to achieve. Remember, in shooting these types of targets you must bend at the waist to raise or lower the bow. If you merely raise or lower the bow arm, the result will have the same effect as changing the draw length, producing a different anchor point and peep alignment. Bend at the waist and find the proper balance before drawing the bow.

On uneven ground, try to align both feet towards the target the same way as you would on a flat surface. If this is not possible and you have to open your stance for proper balance, make sure you rotate your back and shoulders so they are at the same angle to the target as they would be on a regular shot.

The next time you are on a practice range, look for an irregular surface and practice there. Most archers can score from the flat terrain, but good archers can score on all surfaces because they have learned to shoot from their center of gravity and use perfect balance.

Relaxed Shooting

Shooting an arrow and hitting the 10 ring is like solving an algebraic equation. There are a lot of steps to follow if you want to do either with consistency. Aiming is merely one of the steps in the equation of good shooting. Once it is learned, it should become a subconscious process.

As discussed in a previous section, the aiming process starts before you draw your bow and stops after the arrow hits the target. Focus on the exact spot that you want your arrow to hit, place your sight pin on it and draw the bow. If you draw the bow with the sight pin several feet from the target, it requires more muscle movement and time to get the pin on the bullseye. The extra muscles used to move the pin will now have to be relaxed in order to execute a good shot. After you are at full draw, relax all of the muscles except those necessary to maintain a steady, straight-forward push on the bow arm and the muscles of the back that move the release arm backwards.

Many people tell me that they have trouble identifying

the muscles they are to use for the back pressure on the release arm. Try relaxing the shoulder and arm muscles when at full draw. Now act as if you want to hit someone who is behind you with your elbow. These are the same muscles you will use to draw your release arm back, releasing the arrow.

Once your pin is on target and all of the muscles unnecessary for the shot execution are relaxed, start the back pressure for the release. As the back pressure begins, the pin movement decreases and the pin appears to "lock on" the target. Most bad shots are made because the archer fails to maintain back pressure. When this happens the bow arm moves, resulting in a weak shot.

While focusing on the dot, allow your sight pin to settle in on it before starting the back pressure. Nearly all of the top archers focus on the target, not the pin. If you focus on the pin, it will be like following a bouncing ball. The size of the end of the sight pin or the dot on a scope and the magnification of the scope vary with different archers. The best rule is to shoot the combination with which you feel the most relaxed as you aim. Remember, the smaller the sight pin and the higher the magnification of the scope, the more movement you will see when aiming.

The duration of aiming time differs from archer to archer, but not from shot to shot by the same archer. In other words, if an individual releases his arrow eight seconds after coming to full draw, nearly every shot he shoots will be executed within that time frame. This is part of an individual's rhythm and should be maintained for good shooting form.

When shooting 3-D targets, you must train yourself to focus on the imaginary dot that is located in the center of the 10 ring. Concentrate on that spot and allow the pin to settle on it. Relax all tense muscles unnecessary to the shot, apply back pressure, and release the arrow. Keep focusing on the imaginary dot until after the arrow has hit the target. As previously mentioned, do not attempt to watch your arrow flight because that will require you to move your head and will result in a poor shot.

Do not rush the shot; instead, try to maintain your normal shooting rhythm. If negative thoughts enter the thinking process or you lose your concentration, do not shoot. If you hold at full draw too long, do not shoot because your muscles will begin to tighten. Lower the bow and start over. It is impossible to hold the pin motionless, so try to hold it as close as you can to the imaginary dot. The more relaxed that you can keep your muscles, the less movement will appear with the pin. Focus on the spot you want to hit, but concentrate on the steps of your shooting sequence. Again, aiming is just one of the segments in the equation of shooting a good shot with good form.

Program Your Mental Computer

A friend of mine recently purchased a new computer. It is one of the most up-to-date pieces of technology on the market. This marvelous machine can accomplish amazing multimedia tasks with great speed, memory and up-graded features. Modern computers are making our work and play more efficient, productive, and fun in all phases of our lives.

As archers we have access to the most elaborate computer yet developed – the human brain. It will operate almost any program placed into it. If programmed and used correctly, your brain will help you achieve amazing results and is guaranteed to help you raise your tournament scores.

Our daughter Sally has successfully served on world teams and 20 years with the United States Archery Team. When she was younger, she was scheduled to fly to California for the Junior Olympics National Championship. Having a very busy summer, it was difficult for her to put in the practice time she desired. As she was awaiting her departure, she was focusing on the upcoming competition. I told her to take advantage of the flight time and use it to practice. At first she did a little double-take and seemed puzzled by what I was suggesting. I went on to explain that she should get into her seat and concentrate on mentally shooting hundreds of arrows.

That is exactly what Sally did. For the next several hours, she disciplined herself to shoot several hundred shots, visualizing each one from the moment the arrow was out of the quiver until it settled into the 10 ring. She visualized the target and she imagined herself shooting each arrow with perfect form. Every arrow was shot following her normal step-by-step shooting sequence. By the time she arrived at the tournament, she was confident and relaxed. Following a solid performance, Sally ascended the podium to receive the title of Junior Olympics National Champion.

Make no mistake about what I'm saying here. I am not suggesting that mental practice is better or will even replace the necessary hours of physical preparation required to shoot well. In Sally's case, she had been shooting regularly for years and her muscles were well trained. What this experience does show, however, is that a sound mental program with hard physical practice is a difficult combination to beat.

How do you program your brain? First, develop a step-by-step shooting sequence with which you shoot *every* arrow. Use it in practice and in tournaments and don't shoot *any* arrow without concentrating on each part. Try to limit the process to around three steps. When you have free time in your daily schedule, visualize a target and yourself using good form. Follow your shooting sequence and see your arrow hitting the 10 ring.

Most of the Olympic athletes are taught to visualize themselves having a perfect performance of their sport. With enough repetition, their subconscious minds register the performance as a real occurrence. When this is done in archery, it instills the perfect shot in the mind of the athlete. When that archer addresses the target, the subconscious mind says, "This is the same shot on which I have scored a 10 hundreds of times." The archer then routinely follows his or her shooting sequence and calmly executes another 10.

When my friend's computer is programmed properly and the correct data is input, it will accomplish amazing tasks and help him successfully attain his goals. Likewise, as long as the mind is occupied and concentrating on the shooting sequence, a shot with perfect form is almost always the result. Good concentration does not permit negative thoughts or apprehensions to enter into the thinking process. Whenever there is an important competition or a decisive shot like a sudden death shoot-off, don't think about the tournament or the significance of the shot. Instead, replace these thoughts by running your mental program and picturing yourself producing a 10 with perfect form. In doing so, you do not permit anxiety to build and muscles to tighten. To execute a perfect shot, you must stay relaxed and focused. A good mental program will enable this to happen.

Shoot a "Forgiving" Set Up

The arrow bobbled and weaved its way along an erratic flight path from the bowstring all the way to the target where it embedded itself into the 10 ring.

"Good shot. You got it!" congratulated one of my shooting companions.

With a nod of my head, I accepted his compliment. Actually, the shot was terrible, and I knew it. I lost my back pressure and my release hand went out instead of dropping back behind the arrow upon release.

One of the tricks to consistently scoring well is to have your equipment set up so it is as "forgiving" as possible. Forgiving means having your equipment tuned to tolerate small errors in form and execution that will have the least possible effect on the outcome of the shot. If my equipment had not been forgiving, my arrow probably would not have hit the 10 ring.

Making your setup as forgiving as possible is time-consuming, taking a lot of patience and experimenting; but the end result is that your equipment works for you. Any equipment setup will allow you to hit the 10 ring on every shot, if each shot is exactly the same. The problem with archers is they are human and not machines. It is impossible to shoot *every* shot identically.

For a compound shooter, the first step to making your bow forgiving is to make sure the wheels on the bow are in perfect time when at full draw. This usually requires another person to either draw the bow or check the timing. A bow that is not in perfect time is highly critical to any variation in back pressure.

The arrow rest is also very important. You need a rest that will allow for good vane clearance and is sensitive enough to prevent unwanted vibration from being transmitted to the arrow shaft. There are basically two kinds of arrow rests: launcher and shelf types. The launcher style is most commonly used by release-aid shooters. Over the years, I have noticed that most archers tend to set their launcher rests so they are too stiff. A stiff rest will perform adequately, but is not forgiving. A lighter spring tension will absorb more of the shock and vibration from the launching arrow when a poorly executed shot is made. Lighter tension settings will minimize arrow wobble as the arrow leaves the bow. Paper tests may be used to adjust arrow rest settings by shooting arrows through taut paper until the arrow makes a perfect "bullet hole" through the paper. Fine-tuning can be done later.

Shelf-type rests are commonly used by finger shooters and also by some release-aid shooters. To adjust this rest, I prefer using the bare shaft method. If you are right-handed, the bare shaft should impact at about one inch low and left of the fletched arrows at 20 yards. The impact would be low-right for left-handers. Again, fine-tuning is completed afterwards.

Once initial adjustments are made, fine-tuning is done with the tiller. Start out with zero difference in tillage between the top and bottom limbs. Reduce the poundage on the top limb by a quarter of a turn at a time. Each time the tillage is changed, shoot a group of arrows and record the results. When the group opens up, stop and take the tillage back to zero. Now go to the bottom limb and add a quarter of a turn at a time and test. When the group opens up, stop. Now study the results to see where you were getting the best grouping and set your limbs at that setting.

Arrow selection is critical in creating a forgiving archery setup. Arrow manufacturers have spent thousands of dollars developing charts so you can select the proper shaft size. Go to the charts and choose the best shaft for your equipment. For 3-D shooting, I prefer the point weight to be at least 12% front of center (FOC). Three-D shooters want speed, so some archers reduce point weight in an effort to obtain more speed. However, a point weight that is too light may yield speed at the expense of accuracy when performing in wind or when a shot is poorly executed. A heavier point will pull the arrow through the air, minimizing the adverse effect. To determine just how heavy a point to use, you should test several different sizes. Remember, heavier point weights will weaken the spine of your arrow shaft. All testing should be done at the average distance at which you shoot. For 3-D practice, this is usually 35 to 40 yards.

Control of the arrow in flight also helps make your shots more forgiving. Experiment with different sizes and materials for fletching, such as plastic vanes, feathers, and Spin Wings. You will find they make a significant difference in arrow grouping. No one material or size is ideal for all applications, so you need to find the one that is best for your equipment and the way you shoot it. Fletching that causes too much drag will result in a fast wobble in the tail of the arrow and will also reduce your down-range arrow speed. Too little drag will produce a slow wobble in the arrow and is very critical in shooting. Testing will indicate what is best for your setup. To see how the arrow is performing, have someone stand behind you and watch it with binoculars.

Even your bowstring can contribute to making your equipment more forgiving. Different string materials will create a difference in arrow flight, as will the number of strands in the string. Generally speaking, a fewer number of strands will cause your arrows to fly faster but will also permit your string to oscillate more, which can produce a loss of accuracy. Experiment with several different strings to find the one which works best.

Over the years I have found noticeable differences in the performance of arrow nocks. The first thing to remember is that your nock should fit the string snugly, but not tightly. If your nock is too loose or too tight, you will find it much more difficult to shoot small groups. Also, nocks wear out; if your nocks become loose with wear, replace them. Sometimes the fit of the nocks can be fixed by re-serving the string with a different diameter serving material. For shorter length bows, make sure the nock has a deep throat that will remain seated when at full draw. Again, only testing and experimenting will give you the answer as to which nocks work best for your equipment.

The way the bow fits in your hand, as well as the balance of the bow, can also contribute to how forgiving it is. If different grips are available for your bow, try several of them. A grip may be thin or fat and it may be one which has you holding the bow in a high-wrist position or a low-wrist position. You will find one which feels best for you and which enables you to shoot with the most accuracy. There are also a variety of stabilizers on the market. The length, weight, and type of stabilizer can have a significant impact on the placement and tightness of your arrow groupings. Testing and experimenting with these pieces of equipment is also recommended.

Many times we get our bow so it is “close” and then we are afraid to change anything on it. Do not be afraid to try something different. If it does not work, you can always change it back. Analyzing different accessories and equipment configurations is great practice. It helps you get to really know your equipment and how it is going to perform, which provides knowledge that is necessary in different and unusual shot situations. Another advantage of experimenting and testing is that it forces you to concentrate on good shot execution in order to obtain valid results.

Finally, testing helps take the boredom out of practice. I can guarantee that the top archers spend considerable time testing and making sure their equipment choices are the best possible combination for them. If your equipment is forgiving, your mental attitude will be stronger and your scores will be higher!

Stay Relaxed

"What are you frowning about?" one of my friends asked. It was four hours before my line time to start an IBO World Championship.

"I was thinking about those mountains," I replied. "There could be some really interesting shots out there today."

"You spent the whole week practicing hill shots. If you're not ready now, you never will be," he countered. Then it hit me. I was getting tense and my muscles were tightening. It was time to start my mental program and *relax.*

I am sure most of the archers at the World Championship were experiencing the same tension I was having. Why were we feeling this way? We had allowed a combination of things to occur. First, doubts about our upcoming performance became part of the thinking process. An archer, like any other athlete, must guard against negative thinking. Archers entering a competition *must* focus on positive thoughts to be successful. One technique is to keep your mind occupied with other things until it is time to compete. Then, concentrate on shooting good form. Anticipating the awaited tournament is certain to raise your anxiety level, resulting in tension and tight muscles – a formula for impaired performance. The telltale sign for me was when my friend asked me why I was frowning. A grimace requires tightening facial muscles. That is when I realized my back and shoulder muscles were tensing up as well.

Most of us, if we really put our minds to it, can come up with a multitude of reasons to explain our anxiety before a shoot, especially a major tournament like the World Championship. When we boil them all down, the real cause for anxiety is misdirected thinking. Let's examine some of the more common pitfalls that take control of our minds.

One of the most frequent causes of tournament anxiety is self-doubt or lack of confidence. This is why archers need to practice. Once you have mastered shooting skills on the practice field, you know what you are capable of performing. At tournaments, you simply shoot the same shots you executed in practice – shots you know you can confidently and comfortably make. One of the best examples of this is when you judge the distance to the target. Once you determine the yardage, *believe in your decision*! You cannot execute a perfect shot when you are wondering if your distance estimation is correct. Make your decision and then concentrate on making the shot.

A common pitfall to success is for an archer to focus on winning the tournament. Your focus should be on shooting each shot with perfect form. Your pre-tournament mental preparation should include visualizing yourself shooting each target with your best form. Mentally see yourself shooting uphill, downhill, in bright sunlight, and in deep shadow, each time making the shot with flawless form. Imagine what perfect form is for every shot; describe it for yourself; and tell yourself what it is and how you do it. Make sure you visualize your arrow hitting the center of the 10 ring each time. This mental visualization will enable your subconscious mind to activate your muscles in familiar, comfortable patterns. The process will reinforce your form and give you a mental picture of the tournament.

Another trap some archers fall into is watching the score card during the tournament. These shooters become overly concerned with their points. Once the score is recorded on the card, forget that target and start preparing for the next shot. When the shot is done, it is done. Rehashing the previous target(s) will not change your score. The target you are preparing to shoot is the most important one on the course and should receive all of your attention.

Some archers succumb to yet another mental pitfall – misdirected competition. Competition is good. It is how we motivate ourselves and measure improvement. Winning archers also understand they shoot for themselves and compete with themselves. If you are shooting to "beat a buddy" or to impress your friends, you are destined to hurt your performance because your thoughts and focus will be misdirected. You owe it to yourself to shoot the best shots you are capable of making, so concentrate on your objective. How many times have you heard someone ask, "I wonder how Joe is doing today? If I'm going to win, I know I have to beat him." This is just not the case; the only person you have to beat is yourself. Stay relaxed and focus on your shooting because there is not anything you can do to change any score except your own.

Perhaps you have managed to avoid these common pitfalls on your trail to the winner's stand, but you realize you are still tense. How can you relieve this tension and relax? Some basic exercises can help.

The first step in relaxing is to regulate your respiration rate. Short, rapid breathing increases your pulse rate, a symptom of anxiety. To slow your pulse rate, take a deep breath and tighten all your muscles, tensing up your entire body. Now, slowly let all the air out of your lungs and at the same time concentrate on relaxing every muscle in your body. Next, slowly take another deep breath – filling your lungs with air. As you exhale, relax your muscles even more. Repeat this process two or three times; and each time you complete the exercise you will feel your body relax and reach another level of calmness.

Once relaxed, it is important to keep your positive focus on the shot that is in front of you. Try to stay in "your own little world," thinking in terms of no one but you and the target; all else ceases to exist. This is accomplished by permitting your mind to be occupied with only thoughts of the shot process. Focus on using perfect form and then execute that shot.

Practice! Practice! Practice! These mental exercises must be incorporated into your training regimen. They will become an integral part of your shooting only if you develop them on the practice field because this is where you learn mental control. The techniques you use in training are the same techniques you will perform during a tournament. When you have learned to relax and stay relaxed, you have mastered one of archery's biggest challenges.

Clean Up Your Bow Arm for Tighter Groups

During the second day of the NFAA Indoor Championship an archer once walked up and said, "Thanks, Terry. I listened to what you said yesterday and shot my highest score ever today."

"You are going to have to help me out," I said. "I don't remember your name."

"We've never met before," he explained. "I was shooting next to another archer on the practice range and overheard you working with him. I listened while you were helping him clean up his bow arm, so I did the same thing."

The most important part of the shot is the bow arm, where over 90% of the misses occur. True, the reason for a bad bow arm can originate from another flaw in form, but a good bow arm can still save the shot. Whenever an archer is having a problem grouping arrows, he or she should immediately look at this part of the form to correct the problem. The bow arm has to react exactly the same on every shot in order to maintain a tight group.

For the bow arm to perform the same during every shot, it has to be set the same way before the shot explosion. First, the bow shoulder has to be relaxed and set in a low position. If you have tight muscles and the shoulder is high, the shoulder is being held up by the muscles. Can you maintain that shoulder position with the same degree of muscle tension every time? Probably not. That is why the groups will open up. Feel the placement of the shoulder when it is in a down position and you do not have tight muscles supporting it. This is where your shoulder should be when you are executing your shot.

Next is the bow arm. It can be straight or slightly bent if you shoot a compound bow. If you are a recurve or longbow shooter, straight is the main option. The bow arm should be relaxed in either case. Unnecessary tight muscles in the bow arm or bow shoulder will produce bow and sight movement. The only muscle tension in the bow arm should be the muscles needed to maintain a steady force on the bow handle, pressing it toward the target. It is very important that the same degree of forward pressure is applied on every shot or you will experience high or low groups.

When the arrow is released, the bow arm should break directly toward the target at the same angle on every shot. This is a *must*. If it doesn't, you will be pushing or pulling your arrow in another direction. Set up a video camera about 15 feet in front of you when you are practicing. Shoot 10 shots without moving the position of your feet. Play back the video and see how your bow arm reacts. If you are using perfect form, it should react identically every time.

I always have maintained that you can make a lot of form errors, yet still save the shot as long as you have a good bow arm. Clean up this part of your form and your groups will become tighter.

Chapter 3. Attitude – Be Mentally Strong

Attack the Target

Several years ago on the final day of the World Championship, I watched one of my students shoot an 8 on the first two targets. I called him over and instructed, "You got here by shooting a strong, aggressive shot. Now, you are letting the situation intimidate you. Be aggressive and attack the target!"

At tournaments, many archers have difficulty believing in themselves. They will shoot strong shots with perfect form on the practice range, but when the self-inflicted pressure starts to mount, they alter their shot. The target becomes an intimidating influence because the archers put a more significant value on each arrow, and suddenly the emphasis is on the ability to score. When this happens, they try to fine-tune the sight. This adds several seconds to the normal shooting rhythm and the bow arm will either breakdown and shoot a weak shot, or tighten up and produce an erratic explosion.

One must be able to confront the pressure situation with aggressive confidence. As an archer, you must believe in your ability to execute the perfect shot. This self-assurance comes from quality practice. Raise the value of every practice shot and the concentration level needed to execute it. In training, do everything both physically and mentally to simulate a tournament shot. As your skills become refined and the groups grow tighter, your confidence will increase. Place your trust where it belongs, which is in your ability to execute a shot with perfect form.

Rhythm is also critical. Adding extra holding time to the shot rhythm can produce a breakdown in form. If the pin does not settle in, let the bow down and start over. Do not force the shot. When practicing, work hard on maintaining a consistent rhythm. A common complaint from most archers is that they cannot keep a good rhythm in a tournament because their release will not go off or perhaps the arrow does not come through the clicker. Most amateurs as well as professionals add one to two seconds to their normal shooting rhythm when starting a big tournament. This is not a desirable occurrence, but do not compound the problem by getting upset. The dilemma is caused by tension and tight muscles and getting upset only magnifies the issue. Relax and concentrate on the perfect shot. If the shot sequence is a little longer than normal, accept it and make sure you perform the best shot that you are capable of shooting. The rhythm will become a little quicker as you become more relaxed. In practice, try to simulate the start of a big tournament. Add a couple seconds to your normal shooting rhythm, so you will be able to handle it if it happens in a competition. Do not over-aim! Trying to guide the sight pin produces more tight muscles and additional sight movement. Let the pin float, accept the extra movement and shoot a strong aggressive shot. Trust and believe in your form and the arrow will hit its mark.

Have Confidence in Your Shot

Confidence is a factor that separates many archers from being one of the contenders and being a champion. Self-assurance allows the archer to relax and concentrate on making a shot with good form. Without this trust, the mind usually runs negative thoughts and dwells on the outcome of the shot rather than the execution.

How do you develop confidence? You do it by working hard! This is why we practice – because practice will prove that you can make the shot. A great archer does not have a weakness. He or she will work on every type of shot and condition that can be faced on a course, mastering uphill, downhill, side hill, open field, dark tunnel, and across water shots. He or she should be comfortable when shooting in poor light, bright light, rain, fog or wind. This is accomplished by training in all of these conditions until they are mastered. Most people do not like rehearsing the more difficult shots because their groups open up. When faced with these situations in tournaments, the confidence in their ability erodes and the negative thought patterns lead the archer down the path of disaster.

Should your confidence come from shooting a 10 or winning? No! Your confidence should be in the performance, not the result of the performance. It should be in your ability to execute a shot with perfect form. If you can do that, the shot will be the best one that you can produce, which will enhance your chances for a 10. No archer can shoot a 10 every time, but some archers can shoot with nearly flawless form every shot. These are the champions.

The best way to describe the level of confidence that I would like for my archers to have is self-assurance on the verge of arrogance. The arrogance should be in the mind and not in the mouth. In other words, I like arrogance that does not show. No one likes being around conceited archers that flaunt their ability; their performance will reflect their ability. You should have unquestionable confidence in your capability to shoot a shot with perfect form under all conditions and know that you can remain focused on the shot execution, not the outcome of this performance.

You gain the confidence of a champion by being prepared. The equipment should be set up and working properly; and you should have practiced to the point that you know you can shoot every arrow with the very same form. If you are training for a 3-D tournament, you should have practiced yardage estimation until you have confidence in your ability to accurately figure yardage. You should practice mental imagery so that you know you can remain focused under pressure and your attention is directed solely at the arrow that you are preparing to shoot (see **Mental Imaging** pg. 108).

Only one person can put pressure on you and erode your confidence, and that person is you. When you let external stimuli like winning or scoring take on a higher priority, then you start questioning your ability. These typical thought patterns do not become a problem until they are given more importance than executing a perfect shot. You cannot control how another archer will perform, but you can control your performance. Concentrate and focus on making a flawless shot; then you will do the best that you can do. You cannot ask any more than that of yourself. If your performance is not good enough to win, and that is what you want, then you need to raise your level of ability. I would suggest that you focus your practice on any area that costs you points or seek help from a professional coach.

If you are only scoring 80% tens in practice, do not be unrealistic and expect 90% in a tournament. Strive to shoot and perform as well as you do in practice. Most archers who are upset when they come off the tournament course are that way because they knew they could and should have done better. Train and have trust in your ability to duplicate the practice shot, which will help you achieve to your ability. Confidence and focus produce good shots, and good shots produce a top performance.

Self-Discipline

"You knew that shot wasn't going to be any good. Why did you shoot it?" I said, coaching one of my students.

He replied, "I thought I could make it anyway."

How often have you released an arrow and then said to yourself, "I knew I shouldn't have shot it?" How many times at the end of a tournament have you commented, "I would have had a great score if it were not for a couple of bad shots?" The answer is probably "too many."

One of the most important characteristics of a great archer is self-discipline. If the shot isn't there, he or she does not shoot it. When the shot process breaks down due to negative thoughts entering the thinking process, you need to lower your bow because a breakdown in form is sure to follow. Sometimes the shot sequence just does not feel right. If this happens, something is wrong and the odds are the results will be disappointing. When negative thoughts are telling you the shot is not going to be good, listen to them.

Self-discipline is learned on the practice field. Do not ever release an arrow when the shot sequence breaks down – not even at a blank bale. By forcing yourself to stop the shot, you will learn the self-discipline it takes to let down during a tournament.

An attorney I coached from Louisiana asked me, "How do I keep the demons out of my head so I don't have to let down so much?" You have to develop a positive mental picture of your form. This is accomplished by hours of practice, so you will be able to produce the same shot consistently. An archer has to develop confidence in using good form and not the ability to score. Visualization is another beneficial way to practice. Mentally “see” yourself shooting perfect form and this confidence will carry over into the tournaments.

Your concentration and focus have to be directed toward your form. By controlling your form, you can control your shot, which will enable you to shoot the best tournament that *you* are capable of achieving. Note that I did not say anything about score. The final points can vary due to line calls, how steady you are on a given day, or a number of other variables. If you concentrate, stay focused, and use your best form, then you are a winner regardless of the score. In addition, you should only have confidence in your form, not the sight picture or your ability to capture points. Then, when a big tournament or pressure situation arises, the needed confidence will take over and your mental energy will be directed towards shooting a perfect shot.

Control Your Emotions

One of my top archers had just returned from an important tournament and called me. “Well, did you concentrate and shoot perfect form?” I asked.

“I didn’t do very well the first day. I shot a 5 on one of the first targets because it was set four yards farther than the maximum yardage. Then I got mad and out of focus,” he explained.

We discussed the importance of controlling his emotions and keeping his thought process focused. At the next tournament, he carried a 3” x 5” card and read it before he attempted any shot. The card read, “Nothing can make me mad or distract me from shooting perfect form, not even a beautiful woman." He remained focused throughout the tournament and shot 10's and 12's on 39 of the 40 targets.

In order to be a top-level archer you have to control your emotions and thought processes. You cannot let yourself become angry, sad, anxious, discouraged or even overly excited. Your thinking has to be directed at shooting the best shot that you are capable of performing.

The brain is the most valuable piece of archery equipment that an archer possesses and its proper use is what makes a winner. When an adverse situation arises, stop, stand back and look at the circumstance as an outsider. Do not become emotionally involved. If it is something that you can change, then change it. If it isn't, then ignore it and go forward. This is accomplished by visualizing and concentrating on shooting a perfect shot.

A fine example of this was the performance of Ashley Kamuf while competing at the Indoor World Championship in Cuba. The tournament had just started and she had an equipment failure that cost her five points. When the necessary repairs were made, she went back to the line and shot the next 12 arrows into the ten ring. This 16-year-old girl went on to become the youngest female to win the Indoor World Championship. Ashley removed the equipment failure from her thinking and visualized herself shooting perfect form as she waited for the bow to be repaired. When she returned to the line, she went with a positive attitude toward her upcoming performance. The misfortune of the equipment failure was immediately put out of her thinking because it had already occurred and nothing could change the five points that she had dropped. Worrying about it would have only compounded the problem. Instead, she turned the bad situation into a positive one by using the most important piece of equipment – her brain – to focus and capture the gold medal for the United States.

When faced with adverse circumstances … such as equipment failure, missing a target, or perhaps getting mad … don't shoot yourself in the foot! Put it behind you by concentrating your mental energy on shooting the next target with the best form possible. To be a top-level competitor, you have to stay focused and control your emotions.

Don't Give Up on Yourself

At a Junior Olympics National Championship, the top female junior archer in the world was having difficulty the first day of the tournament. The gusty 25-30 mph wind was giving her problems. Her name was way down on the leaderboard and negative talk was present in her conversation with me. It appeared that she was giving up on herself. This is a common reaction for most archers when they are not meeting their expectations. To be one of the best, you cannot let these thoughts or feelings emerge.

At this point I will admit that I lost my cool! I pointed out that you are never a loser as long as you try as hard as you can on every shot. If you think you can shoot shots with perfect form, then you probably will. Every possible point was very important and there was still another day of shooting left.

The next day she faced the tournament with a positive attitude, made up her previous 23-point deficit, and won the title! Two weeks later she went on to win the Junior World

Championships in Sweden during a 40 mph wind.

Win or lose, as long as you give 100%, you should feel good about your performance. Some days the shooting comes much easier than others, but the real winner is the person who thinks positively and gives it his or her all.

Some archers go to a tournament and search for an excuse to blame for their poor performance. Often, they are working on this excuse even before they shoot their first arrow! "I haven't gotten the bow tuned yet," "I haven't had time to practice lately," "I don't feel good today," or "It's too (pick one - windy, rainy, cloudy, sunny, hot, cold) today."

Do any of these sound familiar? I'm sure if anyone looks hard enough he or she can come up with an excuse for a poor performance. Once an archer finds one, then the intensity of concentration will drop because there is something to blame for the bad results that are sure to follow. If this happens, put the blame where it belongs. You gave up on your ability and yourself. You were a quitter.

Learn to shoot with humility. If you don't perform well at a tournament, then say, "I didn't shoot well today." Later, try to identify the problem and correct it so it does not happen again. If you constantly strive to make the weakest part of your game the strongest, before long you will discover that you are a very good archer.

Most tournaments are won or lost because of the competitor's attitude. There are probably more tournaments won by the archer who is in second, third or fourth at the halfway point than by the person who was leading. Why? When the leader makes a mistake, he or she usually begins to focus on the mistake, which compounds the problem. The person who is trailing usually thinks positively and concentrates very hard so he or she will have a chance to win. Leading or trailing, have a positive attitude. Give each shot the best that you have to offer. You owe it to yourself!

Build a Positive Attitude

Several years ago, I went to a 3-D tournament where the people coming off the course were making statements, such as, "This is ridiculous. I thought I was going to run out of arrows. This was the hardest course that I have ever shot."

As I approached the first target, some friends greeted me and declared, "This is your type of course – long shots and small targets."

One of the archers in my group quipped, "Why do you like a course like that?"

"It's challenging and fun," I responded. "You can learn a lot from a difficult course."

To be a top-level archer, you must have a positive attitude. Positive thinking builds confidence, and in turn, confidence produces positive thinking. The two mindsets feed on each other and grow. To develop this approach, you must have consistency in your performance. Practice is so important because it allows you to learn to replicate your shot. To be successful, an archer needs to release every arrow with the same form, muscle tension, rhythm, and follow-through. With such consistent shot execution come tight arrow groups; and the result is confidence and a positive attitude.

In order to be self-assured, you need to have self-control. If you allow a bad shot to eat on you, it will soon have you as a three-course meal. Forget the adverse situation and fill your mind with positive thoughts about the next target. At that point, the only score that can be altered is the next one that you are going to shoot, so make it your best.

A confident attitude about your ability to perform is relaxing to the muscles and the mind. One of the biggest keys to good shot execution is the ability to remain calm. If your mind is saying, “I can shoot perfect form,” then you stand a good chance of doing so. However, if your mind tells you, “I hope I don’t miss,” then the muscles are more apt to tighten, causing poor shot execution.

One of the most important things to remember about using a positive attitude is to not lie to yourself. If you are addressing a 40-yard turkey in a breeze, I do not recommend that you tell yourself you are going to “10” it. Yes, you can think you really would like to capture the 10. But realistically, hitting the bullseye at that distance, knowing the exact yardage, and having no wind would still be challenging for any archer. I prefer to stay upbeat, telling myself that I’m going to shoot perfect form and make the best shot that I can. I would be lying to say I can hit the 10 ring because my mind would then respond, “Who are you kidding?”

Perhaps you are starting the first end of an NFAA Indoor Championship and you feel nervous tension. I do not recommend that you tell yourself that you are calm. Be realistic and acknowledge that everyone is a bit jittery. Enjoy the excitement because this is what it’s all about. Then try to relax your muscles, think positively, and focus on your ability to execute perfect form. Keep the ideas in your mind realistic so you do not dispute them with negative thoughts.

If you can finish a tournament feeling pleased about your performance, even though you did not win, then you have what I call a good, positive attitude. If you are not happy about your game, would you have felt better to have scored 10 points less, but won? Strive to shoot the best that you are capable of doing that day. If your results come out on top, be happy. If not, be glad that you did as well as you could. These feelings will carry forward to the next tournament and will have a positive effect on how you shoot.

When you go to a tournament, your head should be filled with encouraging thoughts about the competition in front of you. If it is rainy, windy, hot or cold, such factors should not be treated as negative influences on your upcoming performance. These same conditions are going to impact everyone else, and the archer who is least affected mentally will become the winner. The person who is standing around complaining is making excuses for a poor performance that is sure to follow. I prefer to think of such hindrances as challenges. I realize that I will not score as high as I would under perfect conditions, so the trick is to accept it and shoot the best score that I can given the situation. The archer with a poor attitude usually has trouble dealing with the lower results and gets down on his or her game. Archery can break the spirit of a weak person, but the mentally strong will stand in the winner's circle.

Calm Down or Pump Up?

A very talented, several-time world champion archer came up to me at a tournament and asked if I would help her because she had not been performing well this past year. After talking and watching her shoot, the main problem was evident. I told her, “You have mastered mind control so well that you have become flat.”

“What do you mean?” she asked.

I replied, “You are too calm and need to pump yourself up so you can perform at top level.”

People are always concerned about the degree of nervousness they experience at big tournaments and how it affects their performance. If you are one of those archers who have mastered mind control to the degree that you experience little to no nervousness, you might be hindering your game. Learn how to “pump up” and raise your emotional level to where you can have a peak performance. Talk to yourself in a positive manner and be energized. For example, I tell myself, “Shoot strong form,” “Attack the target,” or “This is going to be my best shot today.” Even the archer who starts a tournament a little too nervous can easily become flat near the end when he or she starts to get tired and complacent. You need to recognize it and psych yourself back up for the remaining targets. Talk to yourself; control your emotional level; and you will control your performance level.

Why do some archers shoot their highest scores at big tournaments while others have their worst performance? The answer is how their individual personalities deal with and control their emotions. Most people perform at their best when they are pumped up and a little nervous. The key word is a “little.” Being nervous is great, but being tense is disaster.

Nearly every archer is somewhat anxious and nervous

at an important tournament. Harnessing and controlling the degree of this nervousness is the key to success. When an individual is a little edgy, the senses are keener and the muscles react better. This is good for having a top-level performance. However, feeling tension is bad because tension blocks the muscles and mind from executing a fluid shot; and the results will be evident in arrow groupings. High levels of tension and anxiety will take over the mental process and replace a confident shot execution with negative thinking. The archer will no longer be able to concentrate and shoot the way he or she has in practice – and valuable focus will be lost.

Archers need to recognize the degree of nervousness at which they perform at their optimum level. Think back to one of your best tournaments and try to duplicate that level of emotions. Then, recall one of your worst games and try to identify your feelings at that time. Undoubtedly, you will remember that your muscles were very tight and your mind was not focused on the shot execution during this event. It was like a stranger shooting your bow. You must identify your ideal level of nervousness; then work toward bringing your emotions to that point.

The most common problem is when an archer builds anxiety to the height that he or she becomes tense. You can recognize the symptoms of increased pulse rate, rapid shallow breathing and tight muscles. When these signs occur, you need to take control and reverse the process before disaster strikes. You must calm down, slow your breathing and change your thinking. You must remove your mind from the situation causing the anxiety. Visualize the target with your arrow in the middle of the 10 ring and start relaxing your muscles. Mentally begin shooting the target with perfect form and "see" your arrow hitting the bullseye. Continue this process until you achieve the emotional level at which you function best. Your mind should only think positive thoughts about the task in front of you, which is shooting a shot with perfect form. Keep your mind on this track and your arrows will follow a straight path to the 10 ring.

Develop the Power of Focus

I was at a field tournament and the first target was an 80-yard walk-up. The stake for this target was very close to the registration and concession stand. Yes, it was located where the whole crowd could observe the archers start the tournament and they were all watching. This target had all the makings for a real nerve-tester. There was a brisk crosswind as a young man went to the stake for his first shot. He drew the bow and immediately released the arrow when his hand hit the anchor. The arrow soared over the target and the young man sheepishly retreated from the stake. He walked over to me and said, "I don't know who shot my arrow. I don't remember doing it."

"Were your thoughts on the crowd instead of the shot?" I inquired.

He replied, "You know they were."

We have all been there. The same thing happens, but in a milder form, when you fail to maintain back pressure during a shot or perhaps when you jerk your head up to see where your arrow is going to hit. When something like this happens, we usually ask ourselves, "Why did I do that?" The answer is simple. You let your concentration stray from the task that you were trying to perform.

If someone offered you $100 if you could hold a penny

one foot above a coffee cup and drop the penny into it sixty times in a row, would you concentrate really hard on what you were doing? In comparison, do you focus that much during each of the shots at a target tournament? If not, I suggest that if you raise your level of concentration, then you will also raise your score. Focus your attention on the task in front of you, which is to shoot each shot with the best form that you are capable of achieving.

How do you develop the power of focus? First, you have to force yourself to become totally involved in the events of the moment, which is the execution of a perfect shot. You cannot think in the past, such as the bad shot you had on the last target; nor can you think in the future, such as how the score on this target will affect your winning. You must think in terms of the present moment and become completely involved in your shot sequence.

Focus starts before you draw your bow. You must relax and focus your vision and concentration on the exact spot you want your arrow to strike. Next, force your mind to become a meaningful part of the shot process. Remember, all you are doing is identically repeating the same form that you have done thousands of times on the practice range. If you place a more significant value on a tournament shot by thinking, “I have to hit the spot to win,” then your muscles will tighten and you will be unable to replicate the form you use on the practice range.

It is easy to get lost in thought and reflect on ideas that are not part of the task in front of you. When your mind strays, stop and bring it back to the moment. If there was one word that best describes mastering the skill of archery, it would be discipline. You have to discipline yourself and control your thought process. Mental imagery is a good way to practice effective concentration. Visualize and sense each step in shooting an arrow. As visualization and concentration become more vivid, take it to the next level. Do it in front of your favorite TV program or perhaps when you are in a room filled with people. As you become more efficient at controlling your thinking, you will discover there is nothing in the room except you and your focused thoughts. Developing this mindset will help raise your level of performance the next time you shoot before a crowd.

Practice and believe in your visualizations and then your actions in tournaments will make them a reality. Use that important piece of archery equipment, your brain, and make it an effective part of your archery game.

Dwell on the Positive

In a favorite story, there was once a little steam engine that tried to pull a big train up a hill. The process began very slowly and then the little engine started repeating to itself, “I think I can, I think I can.” As the railroad cars chugged into motion, the little engine carried the train over the hill chanting, “I knew I could, I knew I could” (Platt and Munk).

At an archery competition, you need to have an upbeat attitude like that of the little steam engine. As you view the tournament and your performance with a “can do” attitude, you increase your chances of staying focused and shooting effective form. What your mind thinks, your body will try to accomplish. Through practice, an archer establishes a consistent form. In competition, it is important to picture yourself executing the same shot that you developed on the practice range. Attempt to feel the muscles that you use when shooting good form. This consistency in shot sequence is what enables you to achieve tight groups away from competition. It is also the same form that will produce tight groups on the tournament field. Dwell on the positive. Remind yourself that you do shoot a good, consistent shot; and that is all you need in order to have a successful performance at a tournament.

When our daughter Sally was a teenager competing in an indoor national championship, she hit a center 10 on her eighth shot. The problem was it was in someone else's target. She looked at me, shook her head, and stood there for a moment to recompose her thought process. Another coach standing beside me asked, "How will she do on her next shot?"

I quickly responded, "I have ten dollars that say it will be a 10 in the right target." The next shot was a bullseye. When Sally came off the line, we talked about how good her form was and the fact that there were over a hundred shots remaining in the two-day tournament. My advice was, "Shoot your great form and you will do the best that you can do." She did and won the championship by one point.

Every archer occasionally makes a bad shot. The effective archer puts it behind himself or herself and follows up with a series of good shots. Rehashing the bad arrow leaves a negative picture in your mind, which will create self-doubt, change your point of focus, and perhaps alter the shot execution. Imagine yourself at the halfway point of an indoor tournament. You have hit twenty-nine of the thirty arrows on the mark. A friend walks up and asks you how you are doing. Are you going to answer, "I missed one," and then follow this with an explanation for the missed arrow? You shot twenty-nine perfect arrows the first half. This means that nearly every arrow was released with perfect form. Why not take the high road and dwell on your success? Positive thoughts yield positive results.

When you think of an upcoming competition, how do you picture your performance? Do you see yourself shooting a strong and rhythmic shot like you do on the practice range? Are you calm and focused? If the answers to these questions are yes, the odds of having a successful tournament are greatly enhanced. I would estimate that over a third of the shooters are good enough to place at most archery events. Ironically, most of these people seldom or never place at a tournament. Why? They have developed their shooting skills, but have done little or no work in developing their mental game. Many archers can shoot, but very few can remain calm and focused in a competition. Developing mental imagery to create a positive approach at tournaments is just as important as the practice of shooting arrows. Nearly all archers have to work at maintaining a positive attitude at competitions. Making a bad shot does not necessarily mean you will lose. It does indicate that you are going to have to work harder to place. Even if placing is out of the question, you owe it to yourself to do well for the remainder of the game. By turning the situation around and shooting your best during the rest of the event, you will be building a stronger foundation from which to launch your next performance. If an archer can maintain a positive attitude concerning his or her ability to execute a perfect shot, the score and tournaments will take care of themselves. Logically thinking, shooting well is easy. All you have to do is remain calm, stay focused, and shoot consistent form. You do it in practice because that is your goal. Keep that objective at the tournament. Be positive and believe in your ability to execute form that will make you successful.

Learn from Defeat

Just two weeks before a Junior World Championship, several of my top archers had come to my home for final preparations. One of the archers was losing her focus and having a very poor performance during the head-to-head competitions. Using a familiar excuse, she placed the blame for her difficulties on the equipment. Stepping away from the group to have a private discussion, I explained that the problem was with her lack of focus, not the bow in her hands. I showed her how to correct the difficulty and asked her to remove "equipment failure" from her thinking. Upon returning to the shooting line with a new attitude, this young lady began performing like a champion. A few weeks later, she won the Junior World Championship.

Too often archers look for something else to blame rather than face the grim truth that they are the problem. I find it very strange that equipment only breaks down during a tournament, or does it? It is much easier to find fault with something mechanical than it is to acknowledge weaknesses in oneself. If an archer does not accept the blame, how is he or she going to identify and correct the problem? When you have a bad performance, do you think you are the only person who experiences this? What about that person who is standing up there getting that first place award? Rest assured that it was no path of rose petals for him or her to get to that position. The archers whom I coach have won over 350 national and world championships. Every one of them will tell you there were numerous bumps and chuckholes in the road to the top. They accepted the responsibility for their defeat, learned from it, and then raised themselves to a higher level of performance.

Mark Spitz was a great Olympic swimmer and everyone had high expectations of him bringing home numerous gold medals in the 1968 Olympics. At the games, his performances fell far short of his abilities. Claiming two medals, he went home devastated but not beaten. After evaluating and identifying his weaknesses, Mark worked hard on them for the next four years. When the 1972 Olympics arrived, the world watched this remarkable athlete redeem himself with a record-setting achievement of seven gold medals and seven world records. As an archer, losing or coming up short of your expectations can also hurt. You need to address the problems and move forward. Rather than sitting back and wallowing in pity, learn from your performance so you can become a winner.

Olympic archer Ed Eliason had been a top competitive athlete for several decades. I remember talking to him following a less than stellar performance at an important competition. He addressed the situation with a positive attitude saying, “You can learn more from a bad tournament than you can from a good one. I think I learned a lot from this one. I’m going to use what I have learned and I’ll be ready for the next one.”

When your performance falters, analyze your game to see where you got into difficulty. Was it nervousness, too much sight movement, a breakdown in form, over-aiming, trying too hard to hit the 10 ring, distractions from the crowd, not feeling comfortable, or perhaps a loss of focus? When you have a bad tournament, instead of looking for an excuse, look for the reason. Then “fess up” to the real weakness and accept the responsibility for it. You cannot correct an excuse, but you can certainly correct a reason! By identifying the problem and acknowledging it, you give yourself the power to remedy it. Every problem is a challenging situation waiting for a solution. Undoubtedly, you are not the first to have faced this difficulty; so if you are unable to solve it, seek help.

Becoming an accomplished archer is not easy, but you can make it to the top more quickly with a positive attitude. Refuse to invest your time dwelling on the negative results of a poor performance. Instead, build on a positive approach that will help you improve. Refuse to give up on yourself or quit giving it 100% during a tournament. When you give up, you are conducting yourself like a loser. When investing your "all" in the shoot and you fall short of your expectations, you are still a winner. This "can do" attitude provides a foundation that allows you to build toward a championship performance. In the end, winners are not born; they are formed. Learn from your mistakes so you can be on a successful path to the top.

Start 'Em Young

Archery was a family sport and a great pastime for my father, Price, my brother, Steve, and me in the early 1950s.

A generation later, our children Vic, Sally, and Dawn developed a love for archery, as they began hitting the tournament trail with both compound and recurve bows.

Gallery of Champions

Braden Gellenthien, a top world-ranking archer, has set 32 world records and won 18 national and 12 world championships.

Jamie Van Natta, one of the world's top-ranking female archers has received 6 world and 22 national titles. Jamie has also set 13 world records, including the FITA World Record.

D. Alberga Photo

F. Thomas Photo

Vic Wunderle has won 2 Olympic medals, finishing in the top 8 of three consecutive Olympic Games. He has also earned 42 national and 8 world championships. In addition to his father, other fine coaches can be credited for helping him become a champion. After capturing the individual silver and team bronze in the 2000 Olympics, Vic received a hometown "ticker tape parade."

Roger Hoyle has won 3 national championships and set 4 world records, including the FITA which he held for 8 years. The FITA World Record with 144 shots is the most coveted of all world records.

Veteran Senior Pro-Shooter Derry Null has earned 26 national and 6 world titles. He demonstrates some of the best form in archery.

Dawn Wunderle Stultz has celebrated 4 national titles with a compound bow and 1 with a recurve. Her power of focus enabled her to compete successfully at the national level.

Her sister, Sally Wunderle Seipp, has captured 18 national and 2 world titles. She has set 7 world records, including 2 FITA World Records. Sally served on the Adult United States Archery Team for 20 consecutive years.

Adam Wheatcroft set 6 world records and won 18 national and 2 world titles. He demonstrated skills as one of the best pressure shooters in the sport of archery.

Ashley Kamuf First brought home 9 world records and earned 28 national and 9 world titles. She won the adult Indoor World Championship in Cuba at age 16.

Hunter Tuveson is shown with his winner's cup from an indoor national championship. He displays excellent focus as a developing archer.

Senior Pro Ken Yeater relaxes after winning an indoor national title. He was voted into the Iowa Archery Hall of Fame because of his commitment to helping other archers.

Hunter Jackson is a dedicated archer, accumulating 10 national championships and a world title.

Ryan Day has enjoyed several national titles and earned the Junior World Championship. In addition to being a talented archer, he is also a great ambassador for the sport.

Terry and Jeanne Wunderle and Sally Seipp are seen cheering for the USA Olympic Archers.

Chapter 4. How to Shoot the Challenging Shots

Hitting the Invisible Dot

On one occasion, I was at a local archery range shooting at a piece of cardboard with a few dark lines and dots on it. Another archer walked up and asked, "What are you doing… blank baling?"

"No," I replied. "I'm practicing for the turkey target tournament."

"I don't understand," he responded.

I went on to explain that it is often difficult or impossible to see the 10 ring on a turkey target. Too often you hear archers say that they made a perfect shot, but it was not where the 10 ring was located. There are markings on the targets that tell an archer exactly where the kill zone is positioned. For instance, three inches below the waddle is the center of the 10 ring on the turkey when it is facing you. There are feather markings on the wing that indicate where it is situated from a side view. The identifying mark is rarely found in the 10 ring, but it is close. You need to memorize its location so you can focus on the center of the aiming point. On 3-D targets, the 10 ring may be straight above or below the identifying mark or it may be at an angle a few inches to the right or left. An archer needs to practice shooting at these invisible dots so he or she will feel confident when faced with the competition shot.

The majority of archers practice for a 3-D tournament by shooting at an orange dot or at a shot-out hole in the 10 ring on their personal 3-D target. This is good, but it will not prepare you mentally for the real thing. How many 3-D targets have an orange dot on them or a dark empty hole? On most targets, you are searching to identify the exact location at which to aim.

Nearly all deer targets have the center of the 10 ring located a couple inches from the curved muscle on the deer's shoulder. To prepare for this, practice shooting at brown cardboard with a faint curved line on it to imitate the shoulder muscle. A few inches from the shoulder line, pencil in a 10 ring. Make it too faint to see with the naked eye, but visible with binoculars. To practice, search to find the muscle line and then try to hit about two inches from that point. This exercise will also make you mentally strong when confronted with a target under poor lighting conditions.

On black targets, such as a bear, it is usually impossible to see an identifying mark other than a blemish caused by an arrow or someone's nock. To prepare for this type of shot, place a nock in a piece of cardboard. Draw in some faint circles at different distances and angles from the nock. With binoculars, identify the circle you wish to hit, aim away from the knock, and then make the shot. Quite often we have seen an archer put his arrow in the 8 ring, but very close to the 10 ring. The next archer will be attracted to the glowing nock like a moth to a flame and put his arrow right beside it. By practicing this "aiming off" technique, the glowing nock will help you rather than be a hindrance. Training in this manner will enhance your confidence and shooting skills when facing the invisible 10 ring in a tournament.

When shooting 3-D targets, do not shoot at the 10 ring; rather, try to hit an imaginary spot in the middle of the 10 ring. This gives you a bigger margin for error. I always had two sets of target flashcards. One set had a small gold dot designating the center of the 10 ring and the other set was clean. I would study the group with dots until I had the location of the 10 ring memorized, and then I would go through the clean ones to check my memory. When addressing a real target, you should be able to identify the exact center of the 10 ring with the naked eye. Then note some aiming aid such as a blemish or knock. Pinpoint the exact aiming location of the 10 ring from the blemish with your binoculars. Keep your concentration and focus on that point as you draw and make your shot. If you try to find that point after you draw your bow, it is more difficult because the peep reduces the amount of light reaching your eye. This means you spend time concentrating on finding the place to aim, rather than concentrating on the spot and making a good shot.

Shooting 3-D is similar to competing in a golf tournament. Every shot is different, so you should practice and be prepared for a variety of situations. One really bad shot can wreck a scorecard. Master the technique of shooting the "invisible dot" and you are another step closer to being a champion archer.

Shooting in the Wind

In one of the NAA Nationals, a young woman whom I coach shot a new FITA World Record under breezy and rainy conditions. The previous days, when the weather was calm and clear, she shot thirty points less. I asked her, "Why is it you shot higher in the wind and rain than you did on the calm days?"

She replied, "I knew I had to concentrate harder on shooting good form or the wind would destroy me."

Wind will destroy the mentally weak. In order to be a good wind shooter, you have to accept these facts: your sight pin will not be steady; your groups will open up; and your scores will probably go down. All archers know these facts are true, but very few are willing to accept the reality of it happening. Then, when confronted with a wind shot, they tighten more muscles in an attempt to steady the sight pin and aim two or three times longer than their normal shooting rhythm. By the time the shot is executed, the bow arm is shaking at about a "6.2" on the Richter scale. The chances of executing a shot with good form have diminished to nearly zero.

The next time you go to a tournament where the wind is blowing be mentally and physically prepared. Of course, the first thing to realize is the same wind that is affecting your shooting is also affecting everyone else's. Scores will be lower than if calm conditions prevailed. Accept this fact and concentrate on making each shot the best you possibly can.

Very few archers practice shooting when it is windy. Why? Mentally and emotionally it is hard for them to accept that their arrow groups are at least three to four times larger than they are under calm conditions. With practice, the arrow groups will tighten, but they will never be as good as they would under calm conditions. Your goal should be to reduce the group size instead of holding every arrow in the 10 ring. Some gusty winds are so difficult that the challenge is to hold the pin within the 8 ring. Be prepared to accept this limitation.

The main trick to shooting in gusty winds is to avoid fine-tuning your shot; instead, concentrate on making a shot with good form. Sometimes during gusty wind conditions you have to hold the bow at full draw longer than you would with your normal shooting rhythm. When this happens to archers, they typically lose back pressure, causing the bow arm to move. The result is a weak shot. If you must aim longer than usual, it is very important that you apply back pressure to the string before releasing the arrow.

During one very windy tournament, I had to hold the bow at full draw for a long time before shooting. The gusty wind was so fierce that it kept blowing the pin off the target. When I did release the shot, the results were respectable. One of the archers in my group asked me how I could hold it for that long and still make a good shot. I explained that I was only pointing the bow at the target and keeping my muscles relaxed. When the wind finally eased up enough for the pin to settle down, I added back pressure and let the shot happen. The wind will beat you if you keep your back muscles tightened while you're trying to fight it and get your pin to settle down.

To learn to shoot in the wind, spend some time at the practice range on windy days. Practice holding the bow at full draw longer than your normal rhythm. When you decide to shoot, apply back pressure to the string. This added force usually locks the pin on the target. If you find your muscles are tightening up, let down and start the shot over.

Many archers face a dilemma when they feel they have to hurry their shot. Often they shoot bows with draw weights that are much too high. Consequently, they cannot hold their draw comfortably; they rush the shot; and they sacrifice accuracy. Shoot only the pounds of draw weight you can comfortably control – not pull.

When considering draw weight, please pay attention to

what is used on children's and youths' bows. Children should never be permitted to shoot the higher poundages. The excessive strain will damage growing bones. Anyone can shoot respectable speeds with a good, well-tuned bow and lighter carbon arrows. Teach children how to make an accurate shot. This is the key to success, not high draw weights and fast arrows.

The next difficulty is arrow drift. Olympic archers have learned to master this problem while shooting arrows from lower poundage recurve bows at targets out to 90 meters (about 100 yards). Nearly all of them shoot equipment designed to minimize arrow drift, such as carbon arrows with Spin Wing or small vanes. This combination reduces the amount of surface area for the wind to hit, thus decreasing the amount of drift. Specialized equipment combined with many hours of learning to judge arrow drift enable them to shoot with much more confidence in the wind.

Three-dimensional and outdoor target archers need to practice during windy conditions so they learn to know how much their arrows will drift. The amount of wind drift varies according to the wind speed, the direction of the wind in relation to the shot, and the distance of the shot. If you find your arrows drift 10 inches when shot at fifty yards in a twenty-five mph wind, then aim 10 inches on the other side of the ten ring. This is called "aiming off." It is an important, although difficult, technique to learn. Resist the temptation to adjust your sight pin to compensate for the wind because the next shot might be in a sheltered area out of the wind. As an example, to hit the 10 ring of an animal target, you may have to be mentally prepared to aim at the shoulder or the back of the lungs. You learn how to make these types of shots on the practice field.

To master wind shots, place your concentration and confidence where they belong. Focus on shooting the shot with the best form that you can use. Prove it to yourself. Place a bullseye target at 30 yards and shoot it on a gusty day. For the first 20 shots, perform the way you normally do under windy conditions and record the score. For the second 20 shots, let the pin float and make sure you execute the shot with good form. If the pin floats out of the 5 ring, do not be concerned. Go ahead and make the shot; just be sure you shoot with good form. Compare the scores and then you will know…*you have to trust your form.*

Mastering the Hills

Many accomplished indoor target archers experience disappointing scores when they begin shooting outside, especially at 3-D or field tournaments. Part of the problem is performing shots from the awkward foot or body positions that are usually encountered. Let's face it. A good course will find an archer's Achilles heel, if there is one.

A good course introduces shooters to uphill and downhill shots, as well as the difficult side hill shots where either your toes or heels point downward. Shooting these types of shots should be mastered on the practice range. Whether they are at a club or on your personal property, most practice ranges, are built on level ground. To become skillful with incline shots, you might want to consider building your own "hill."

You can design your own slope out of two by four plywood lumber. Make the platform 20" wide and 36" long. Elevate one end of the platform with legs so it will stand 8" high. By turning the platform in different directions, you can simulate most of the hill shots you will encounter.

I have discovered the fundamental elements to shooting angle shots are good balance and remembering to bend at the waist. If you do not have perfect balance when shooting the uphill or downhill shots, try moving your feet a few inches closer together. This narrower base usually provides the desired stability. Before attempting the shot, point the bow toward the target the same way you would when shooting on a flat surface. If corrections for good balance are needed, make them now. You may want to use boots or ankle-high shoes, which will add to your stability for the sharper angle shots.

Many times I have watched archers change from their normal straight or slightly open stance to a very open stance. They do this for better balance, but by changing their stance they have altered their normal shooting form. The more open stance changes the angle created by the bow hand, bow shoulder, and release hand. This means the archer will have to anchor further back on the face or push the bow arm out further to maintain the same draw length. Either way, the results will not be consistent. Angle shots should be made with an archer's normal shooting form, except for changing the feet or bending at the waist.

When addressing uphill and downhill shots, an archer must bend at the waist to reach the proper angle. Imagine your back with a rod from your waist to the top of your head and another rod from the bow hand to the elbow of the release arm. This imaginary cross design has to be maintained during all types of shots. If an archer stands erect and merely raises or lowers the bow arm, a good, consistent shot is impossible. It will change your normal draw length as well as the anchor and peep alignment.

The cross design can be achieved in two ways. Some archers bend at the waist before they draw, while others draw the bow and then bend. I personally prefer the latter because I like to make the cross design in the same manner as I would if I were shooting on a level surface. Once I am at full draw, I rotate at the waist until the pin is on the target.

With the aid of the sloped platform, you can work out the best shooting form for yourself. After practicing the different angle shots, you should find that your level ground shooting has improved as well. Once you become comfortable with angle shooting, take a portable practice butt to a hill and test your form. The different angles, as well as the different footing surfaces, do make a difference.

Performing on hills with the sharp angle shots and poor footing is part of 3-D and field competition. Mastering these will help you compete with the top archers.

Plumb Your Body

For many years, Bedford, Indiana, has hosted a top-level competition in its hilly, picturesque countryside. The practice range has been set up on a particular side hill, and every year it is the same. Shooters begin rehearsing at the practice targets, and their arrows are either hitting way to the right or way to the left. Soon the archers begin cranking on their sights as if something terrible has happened to their equipment en route to the tournament.

One time, as I was standing there watching the same scene play itself out, an archer near me made the comment that he was going back to his car for some wrenches. He could not move his sight far enough to bring his arrow groups back to center.

"I wouldn't do that," I suggested quietly. "The problem is you and not the equipment."

"What do you mean?" he asked.

This archer, like dozens of others that weekend, was facing one of the archery demons – shooting on a hillside. The problem was in his form and not with his tackle.

The practice field at Bedford was on an uphill angle. Like a lot of other shooters, this fellow was leaning into the hill and putting all of his weight on his toes. The archers' bodies were hunched over and their shoulders were bent inward. As they released their arrows, one of two things happened. Some of the archers still had a strong explosion as the shot broke, but the bow arm shot left because it was out of line from his or her natural form. In the case of my new acquaintance, he was making a weak shot and the arrow was hitting to the right. He was so far off balance that he was not achieving a strong shot.

Many of the archers were making pin adjustments on the practice range and running into disaster from the very first targets on the competition course. They had mistakenly changed their sights to compensate for their poor form at one particular angle on the practice field. On the competition course, the uphill, downhill and variety of side hill shots simply did not match up with the way they had just adjusted their sight pins. The only shots where they could hit accurately were ones where the angle of the hill was the same as the practice range. And few were.

When shooting on hills, you need to plumb your body to the angle of the ground, at least to the degree that is possible. If you are standing where your toes are uphill, for example, put more weight on your heels and straighten your back. Put your body in a perpendicular line to the plane on which you are standing. Use the same form you normally use, and you will be able to make the same shot without altering your sight settings.

I truly appreciate a good 3-D archer. These skillful shooters have proven that they are not only capable of judging distance, but are also very efficient at aligning and balancing the body to compete on any type of terrain. If you have any weaknesses in your form, an experienced target setter will find it. The good ranges are set with a variety of uphill and downhill angles and standing positions to test your abilities.

Most archers can shoot well on level ground because that is what they practice. But to be a proficient 3-D shooter, you must be able to master any type of foot placement and body positioning that is presented. As noted earlier, a light-weight practice target will help you learn shots on all types of terrain. When you train, simply carry it with you as you move from one slope to another.

Archers have a tendency to practice shots they are successful shooting. Great archers practice their weaknesses to make them stronger. Learn to master the difficult shots, and then you can walk onto the course with skill and confidence.

Believe in Your Yardage Estimations

While I was waiting for my turn at the shooting stake, I studied the small deer target and set the pin for 32 yards. Moments later I second guessed myself and changed the sight setting to 35 yards because I decided the target looked farther away. Now it was my turn at the stake. I figured the distance by one more method and came up with 36 yards. Again I changed my sight setting, this time to 36 yards, knowing this distance would give me a perfect ten. I released the arrow, hitting high in the 10 ring. If I had placed the pin at 35 yards, the arrow would have been neatly centered in the ten. For some, this is where the problem arises.

I was confident that 36 yards was the correct distance so I produced a confident, strong shot with good form. If I had kept my pin at 35 yards, negative, self-doubting thoughts would have crept into my thinking and I probably would not have executed a strong shot. You simply cannot use good form with uncertain thoughts running through your head. When you commit to your yardage estimation, believe in it! You must have trust in your judgment so your mind is free to concentrate on your shot sequence. If you shoot bad form, the chances are great that you will hit either a little left or a little right of where you are aiming. The combination of weak form and a small error in distance estimation can rob you of the 10 point score and you may easily end up with an 8 or worse. A shot with good form and a small error in distance estimation stands a good chance of catching the 10 ring at either the six o'clock or twelve o'clock positions.

How do you develop this confidence and skill? You accomplish it the same way you do with your shooting – by practicing. A good 3-D archer will spend approximately as much time training with yardage estimation as he or she will shooting arrows. Yes, it might be boring; but if you wish to shoot high scores, you must be able to estimate the distance to the target within a yard or two. Being off as little as three yards will put you in the 8 ring.

I personally use several methods for estimating distance; that way I can cross-check, just in case an optical illusion has fooled me. If the first two methods do not agree, I use a third or maybe even a fourth method of judging the distance. The following are some of the approaches I use to teach distance estimation:

Step 1: Begin with a basic method of estimating distances. You must be able to recognize a given distance, such as 30 or 35 yards. Practice until you can look at your surroundings and estimate how far the 35-yard target is from you. A good way to study this is to tie a milk jug to the end of a 35-yard cord and drag it behind you. Look back at the milk jug and get the feel for that distance. Then look at the ground between you and the target and try to identify the same distance. Repeat the process until your estimate can come within a yard of the 35-yard distance.

Step 2: Pick a spot that is 35 yards away from you. Now locate another spot 10 yards closer than the 35-yard mark. Finally, choose a third spot, this time 10 yards farther away than the 35-yard mark. You can practice the exercise by tying a piece of ribbon on the cord at 25 yards. Then tie 10 yards of cord to the milk jug and attach a pop bottle at the end. As you drag the cord using these items, you can learn to judge what a 10-yard span looks like at intervals of 25, 35, and 45 yards. Finally, fine-tune your estimates for distances that fall near one of these yardages.

A way to check your estimate in steps one and two is to locate a mark half-way between you and the target. Figure the distance to that mark and then double it. Using these two estimation methods should put you close to the money. If you come up with the same distance using both estimation methods, you can confidently set your sight and shoot the shot.

If there is a significant difference in the results of these two methods, measure a third way by picking an object that is about 10 yards on either side of your target. With this mark, refigure the distance using steps one and two. Whatever yardage you estimate, believe it and shoot it with confidence and good form.

The following are two general rules:

- Bright light and shadows, as well as the tunneling effect of trees in some of the shooting lanes, can make a target appear closer or farther away than it actually is. Try to concentrate on a tree, bush, or some mark near the target when estimating the distance. This is the way you practiced yardage estimation, so your results should be more accurate.

- Do not shoot uphill and downhill targets at their actual distance from you. A quick method for arriving at the correct shooting distance is to subtract the height (the distance up or down from your horizontal plane) from the length (the actual distance from the target). For example, if the target is 40 yards away, but is 3 yards higher than where you are standing, subtract the 3 yards from the 40 yards and shoot it for 37 yards. The same is true if the target is 3 yards below your horizontal plane.

A 3-D archer can be an accurate shot, but without yardage estimation skills, success will be hard to achieve. To master the sport, dedicate as much time to judging distances as you do to shooting arrows.

Chapter 5. Handling the Pressure Shots

Handling the Bad Shot & Bad Tournament

Years ago, a young girl whom I coached called me after an important tournament to discuss the event and her performance. She was a very talented archer and held several world records. On this occasion she was not pleased with her shooting, finishing third when she was capable of capturing first place.

"I stunk!" she exclaimed, bashing herself.

My response was simple, "Let's examine your performance and see what went wrong. Remember, you can learn more from a bad tournament than you can from a good one. It sounds as if this one can help you in the future."

Every competitive archer and every bow hunter should strive to improve and refine his or her skills of the game. Using each tournament as an opportunity, consider what did you do right? What did you do wrong? How do you correct the problem? How do you prevent it from happening again? Strive to answer these questions after each event. You can learn from your wins, but you can get a better education by examining your losses. As we go through life, we learn a lot of big lessons from the mistakes that we make. Archery is the same kind of teacher.

Having a bad tournament can be a positive thing if you learn from it. First, you need to control your attitude. If you get down on yourself, become angry, or bask in self-pity, then you are a loser and you will continue to lose. Your mind is a powerful tool, creating images of yourself that will control your muscles and reflexes. If you focus on losing, your mind will see you as a loser - and that is just what you will be. Be a winner. If you do not come away from the tournament with the highest scores, examine what went wrong and learn from those things. Go forward with a positive attitude. If you can do this, then you are still a winner. Your mind will see yourself as a success and you will shoot much better scores on the tournament field, while using greater confidence and skill. Treat your mistakes, and the solutions to them, as building blocks for a future championship performance.

Dealing with a bad shot during a tournament can be a little more challenging. To begin you must look at it from the viewpoint of "what went wrong?" Identify the problem quickly so you can take corrective measures and prevent it from happening on the next shot. The most common reaction to a bad shot, and the one that ruins most archers, is thinking how it will affect one's scorecard. If your mind goes in this direction, it will be very difficult to concentrate on making the next arrow "the best shot that you will shoot that day." Everyone occasionally makes a bad shot. Analyze and correct the problem instead of worrying about the effect it has on your scorecard. This practice can actually help you have a better tournament than you would have had without the bad shot. The additional stimuli can force you to concentrate and focus harder on good shot execution. With a positive approach, you can make up for lost points from the "bad arrow," as well as raising the whole level of your performance for the day. There have been many big 3-D tournaments won by an archer who had a zero recorded on his or her scorecard. A missed target does not mean that you will lose the tournament. It only indicates that you need to raise your level of concentration, thus enabling a top performance.

Tournament Nerves – Your Winning Edge

It was a few hours before the start of the second day of the NFAA Indoor National Championship. Our older daughter, Dawn, was tied with another young lady for first place. I instructed Dawn to shoot the final day like it was just another practice session. "Pay no attention to your opponent's score or your own. She'll do enough worrying for both of you. Focus on your form and shoot the best shot possible," I advised. Even though she was nervous, that is what she did…as she captured her third national championship silver bowl.

Over the years, I have watched people nail the bullseye again and again during practice, almost as if they were invincible. Then in the face of an actual tournament, their scores would plummet to fourth or fifth place. Were the winners that much better? I doubt it. In most competitions, the difference between the top score and being "out of the money" is only a few points, generally less than five percent of the possible total. A typical fifth-place archer can consistently shoot first place scores in a practice setting.

Only a few archers ever shoot as well in a tournament as they do in practice. This is true whether they are on the crowded line of an indoor venue or in a spacious outdoor 3-D event. Why? Archers who are flexible and can perform equally well in practice and in tournament settings have learned to control their nerves.

All competitors, including archers, get anxious. This is not the problem. The difficulty arises when you cannot control the effects of stress. Being nervous can actually be beneficial, as the adrenaline charge makes your senses sharper and improves your natural reaction time. Your muscles are more responsive and your performance improves. The trick is to harness this powerful energy source and make it work in a positive manner for you.

How do you accomplish such a feat? Work to develop a strong mental program. Your mind is the source of your anxiety and the manager of this energy. Properly trained and used, it will give you that slight edge that makes you a winner. Unchecked, it will keep you on the sidelines watching others collect the trophies and awards.

The first step is to try to relax. Take a deep breath and do some simple stretching exercises to relieve tension build-up. Take command of your thinking process and the nervousness. Use the benefits of sharpened awareness to your advantage.

Second, think positive thoughts about the shot in front of you. Do not let negative thinking or concern about the competition cloud your mind. Visualize the arrow going into the bullseye or 10 ring, as you mentally see yourself performing the perfect shot. Experience has shown that if you visualize yourself using good form and the arrow hitting the target, your shots will be more consistent and successful. Your muscles will do what your mind tells them to do.

Third, think *only* about the shot in front of you. Develop a routine, focusing your mind on the sequence of steps in that set. For example: 1) seat the bow hand properly, 2) focus on the exact spot you want to hit, 3) let the pin float on the spot, and 4) pull the bow apart and shoot strong. The sequence will vary somewhat from archer to archer, but should certainly include the weakest points of your shooting form.

Thoughts similar to these are the only ones that should be in your mind. If negative ideas are present, let down and mentally go through the shooting sequence again. Then re-address the target and follow your sequence of shooting steps.

There is nothing wrong with letting the bow down. It is wrong when you release an arrow that you think will be a bad hit. Since there is only one chance for each arrow, you owe it to yourself to make it the best one you have to offer.

To strengthen your mental program, place yourself in a variety of pressure situations. Challenge another archer and make practice a competition. A favorite exercise of mine is to allow each archer one shot at a target and increasing the distance by 5 yard intervals. We normally start at 20 yards and end at 50 yards. It is a quick game that teaches the importance of each arrow. You have to learn to pay attention only to your shots while ignoring those of your opponents.

Another effective pressure situation is a novelty shoot at a tournament. The setting provides plenty of spectators and a great deal of commotion. You have to learn to take the crowd out of your mind and focus on the shooting sequence. If you think you are a good shot, believe it and then shoot to prove it.

Before starting a tournament, go to the practice range. Shoot next to one of the best shooters in attendance. This will put mental pressure on you. Remember not to focus on what the other archer is doing. Focus on your own shooting routine.

Finally, participate in archery demonstrations whenever possible. You can perform for a few people or entertain a large audience. You will be honing your skills as an archer and promoting our great sport.

The key to controlling tournament anxiety is to develop a program of strong mental control. Establishing a shooting sequence on the practice field is the most effective way to make your mental game a natural part of your shooting routine. Remember, you learn on the practice field and practice on the tournament field. The best opportunity to test what you have achieved is in competition. The more tournaments you shoot, the better you will be at managing your thinking and stress level. When you master mental control, you have taken the biggest step toward being a champion archer.

Handling Pressure and Distractions

Competing at an indoor target tournament, one of my students performed well with the exception of two shots. When I asked him if he ran his mental program on every arrow, he replied, "Yes."

His buddy who was standing beside us remarked, "He may have been running his program, but he was flipping the channels."

At that moment, the true problem came to light. The archer's concentration was broken by something that was going on behind the line. Instead of letting down and starting over, he continued with the shot. Unfortunately, the results were reflected in his score.

Many things can create pressure or be a distraction. Score, winning, worrying about a competitor's performance, trying to meet the expectations of others, or even your own ego can create such mental distraction that you will lose your concentration. When anxiety rises, focus declines and performance suffers. Needless worry is the greatest hindrance in reaching a top score in an archery competition. I refer to it as “needless worry” because it is nearly always a concern about something that you cannot change. Will agonizing about points or beating the competitors increase your chances of raising your score or cinching first place?

The most important attribute of a great archer or any other athlete is the ability to remain focused when faced with diversions. Everyone gets side-tracked, but the exceptional athletes quickly refocus and unite the bond between their mind and body. Distractions are a part of the sport and so are coping with them. These diversions are not a problem until you let your thinking dwell on them; instead, let them pass and treat them as just part of the game. If you give mental interruptions more importance than your performance, then they will hinder what you accomplish at the shooting line. Actually, distractions and pressure are what make archery exciting. They give us a surge or charge, pump us up, and add thrill to the game. If they didn’t, we would quickly get bored with the sport.

Think of a situation when you lost your cool and your point of focus went south. Replay that event in your mind, but this time think of how you would handle it in a more positive manner. Do not let the distractions get to you and dominate your performance; instead, remain calm and in control. I like to think of diversions as a normal part of a tournament. Look at the circumstances calmly and focus on what you are supposed to do. Stay in control of the situation and do not let what is happening influence your emotions. When you are faced with distractions and you become emotionally involved, step back and observe the situation as an outsider. This will give you a more objective view. If you cannot manage your feelings, you will not be able to focus; and if you cannot focus, you will lose the opportunity of giving a top performance.

At a national tournament, one of my accomplished archers was a bundle of nerves. I called him over and said, “If you really want to see something funny, watch the other shooters. See how nervous they are and what they are doing to themselves.” He started pointing out different contenders, noting the humor in what they were inflicting upon themselves. Then I asked him, “Were you looking at someone else or in a mirror?” He saw the true humor in the situation and laughed at his own behavior. Observing the circumstances as an outsider gave him the insight he needed to address the tournament with a more relaxed approach and have an excellent performance.

Have your friends work with you in practice, letting them distract you as you force yourself to remain focused on your game. Distractions are not a problem unless you let them override your performance at the shooting line. Learn to clear your mind of irrelevant thoughts and free your body of the tension. The body should be relaxed except for the muscles needed to execute the shot; and the mind should be calm and directed at shooting the perfect shot.

On the practice range, I will occasionally bet one of my students a dollar on his or her ability to shoot five spots in a row. Once the person agrees to the bet, I announce the wager to everyone in the vicinity and invite them to watch. This creates a distraction and unwanted pressure; so now my student must take control of the situation, while refocusing on the task in front of him or her. The shooter’s concentration has to be directed at shooting a shot with perfect form, rather than scoring five 10’s.

The next time you encounter an upsetting situation in activities other than archery, force yourself to control your emotions. Try to remain calm and go back to what you were doing before the interruption occurred. I had one female archer who had to give a speech in front of a sizable crowd. She was nervous, so she ran her archery mental program and quickly regained her composure. The athlete had relied on and used mental control in archery so much that she turned to it when another difficult situation confronted her. Practicing mental control in your daily living will enhance your archery performance; but more important than that, it will help you face other circumstances in life.

At an indoor national championship, one of my top-level archers had his release go off accidentally and he shot a no-score arrow. He was mentally down and upset, so I instructed him, "Now show me what you are made of. Get your emotions under control, refocus and clean the rest of the shots." He did, and that impressed me. This type of concentration is what makes a champion. It is good advice to remember that feeling sorry for yourself and giving up is what makes a loser. Sometimes it is very difficult to put a bad shot behind you, but you must try hard to regain your focus. The more you work at refocusing, the easier it will become in the future. Archers train many hours in developing their shooting accuracy. Practicing emotional control and focus under pressure are equally important.

Help Your Body Avoid Stress

At an ASA World Championship, one of my students was speaking with me on the practice range. Noticing he was uptight, I suggested, "Let's walk over here for a while and talk."

Stepping away from the excitement and the commotion, I proceeded to encourage and calm him. When he returned to the field, he downshifted from “high gear” to a more relaxed and methodical approach for the upcoming targets. In competition his performance was at maximum level, as he finished in the top five.

To help your body avoid the stress and anxiety of an important tournament, regulate your sleep, diet and breathing. In the case of the archer at the ASA World Championship, shallow rapid breathing was inhibiting his body from delivering a top performance. The result was an accelerated pulse rate, which produced tension in the diaphragm muscle and increased the level of anxiety. As you face competition, control your intake of air with slow, deep, rhythmic breaths, using the diaphragm muscle. You can feel the muscle expanding the stomach area when done properly. Let the air out slowly. Concentrate on relaxing your neck and shoulders as you do the exercise. Use a key word, such as “relax,” to help trigger a calming effect. Practice this training with archery and in any adverse situation involving work and daily activities. The more you practice the technique, the stronger your archery program will be.

Athletes need to get plenty of sleep the night before a competition. Sufficient rest allows your mind and body to handle pressure situations and avoid anxiety. Try to recall times when you did not have adequate rest. Do you remember your body feeling out of sync or your patience being a little short? If not, maybe you remember your friends and relatives pointing this out to you. Lack of rest will inhibit a top performance.

Proper diet also plays an important role in regulating your body, mood and performance. You want your body to run on a consistent cycle, avoiding highs and lows in your energy levels. High carbohydrate diets lower the blood glucose levels and reduce energy output. This has the effect of making you feel more relaxed and calm. On the other hand, high protein diets keep blood glucose levels elevated, producing more energy. It takes longer for the protein to break down and get into the blood stream. Try to modify your diet so it best fits your performance and personality.

Some people and advertisements promote high carbohydrate liquids and bars for a quick energy boost. These drinks and bars are loaded with simple sugars that get into the blood stream very quickly. Even though they produce quick energy, they have a tendency to drop you physically and emotionally as soon as the body has removed the sugars from your blood.

My recommendation is for archers to eat a high carbohydrate meal, such as spaghetti or pasta, the evening before a competition. These carbohydrates will be in the body to provide energy for the next day. They will also have the tendency to make you calmer and will help foster a good night's sleep.

Breakfast is a different situation. What you consume for breakfast largely depends upon your energy and emotional levels. If you have a long day of archery ahead and you typically run low on energy before the day is through, eat a high protein breakfast such as meat, cheese and eggs. Try to eat breakfast an hour or two before the competition, giving time for your body to break down the proteins.

If your emotional levels run high and you face tournaments with an excessively hyped up personality, my recommendation is a high carbohydrate breakfast such as bagels or oatmeal. Several of my top target archers tell me they have better results with this breakfast because the pin will settle in better. On the other hand, several of the 3-D archers tell me that the high protein breakfast gives them the energy they need to shoot a 40-target tournament. Try each to find which works best for you. Whatever you do, stay away from foods high in caffeine or sugar.

Drinking liquids is a must while competing. Your body is like an automobile that requires fluid for the cooling system to function properly. The body is constantly releasing water, and as it evaporates, the fluid produces a cooling effect. This liquid has to be replaced or you will become sluggish, overheated, or perhaps encounter heat stroke. The rule of thumb I had for my family was that you should have to go to the restroom at least once every hour or you are not consuming enough liquid. As far as the type of liquid to be consumed, I recommend water, fruit juices, or re-hydrating sports drinks that do not contain caffeine or a high level of sugar.

There are many pieces to the puzzle of having a winning game. Adequate rest, controlled breathing, and a proper diet will not guarantee you a first place trophy, but they will improve your chances of performing at your best.

Focus on the Right Things

The second day of competition for an NFAA Indoor Championship was slated to begin in 30 minutes. I was talking with some of my students in the male youth free-style division, as I tried to prepare them for a successful performance in their final leg of the tournament. "You have much better form than you shot yesterday," I cited to two of the archers. "Both of you were focusing on hitting the 'X' because you knew that it would take a good score to win. You have been shooting very tight groups in practice, but you changed and were trying to fine-tune your aiming a little more for this competition. As you found out, it doesn't work. If you want to shoot well today and stand a chance of placing, you have one choice. Put the pin in the center of the white (5 ring) and shoot the best form that you can shoot. Don't try to hit the X ring; try to hit the middle of the white. The archers in the lead usually shoot defensively and their scores often go down. Shoot good form and you might pass them up." I then turned to a student who was standing next to me and said, "You shot 60X yesterday and you won't be coming down to join the others because you have a comfortable lead. Treat today as a practice day and just shoot good form."

With three ends to go, one of the students came to me and said, "I'm hitting an 'X' on the first four arrows, but I always hit a 5 on the last arrow. Why am I missing the last shot?"

I asked him, "Were you trying to hit the white the first four arrows?"

"Yes," was his reply.

I further questioned, "After you hit four 'X's,' were you trying to hit the 'X' on the fifth shot?"

He smiled and answered, "Yes. Now I know what I'm doing wrong." With renewed concentration, the young archer shot clean on the next three ends, finishing with a 300, 52X round. Changing his point of focus raised him to a top performance, as he moved from eighth place to second, behind my other student who had a record-setting finish.

Picture yourself in the following scenario: You are

shooting at an indoor archery tournament against competitors of equal abilities. They are using standard shooting lanes and targets, but your lane is a little different. You have to stand on a piece of four-inch foam with two small tree limbs between you and the target. Your target is not securely fastened, and a fan is blowing on it. There are several obstacles that are definitely inhibiting you from having a top performance, which leaves you at a distinct disadvantage. This type of situation is what many archers unknowingly do to themselves at a tournament. They mentally create obstacles that restrict them from shooting their best game, as they cloud their minds with irrelevant ideas and anxieties. Their thought patterns begin to run in many directions, resulting in a condition of unrest and tightened muscles. Performances are handicapped with distractions, just as they were with the archer in the previous set of circumstances.

The common pitfalls for most archers can be summarized in two words, "win" and "score." Focusing on these prevents an archer from directing the thought process to where it belongs, which is shooting a shot with perfect form. Concepts of winning and scoring have no importance until the competition is over. During a tournament, the focal point has to be on the performance, not its end result. By placing emphasis on "win" and "score," you create unnecessary anxiety. This in turn produces mental distractions that prevent proper shot execution. Once anxiety takes over one's thinking, a negative attitude erodes the ability to shoot a smooth shot. It is important for you to have a positive focus on your shooting skills. These thoughts will then help you become more relaxed and calm, enhancing your performance.

This mental approach, as you well know, is not easily mastered. Not only are you hampered by your self-inflicted pressure, you are also bombarded with the expectations of your friends and relatives. It is important for you to rework your goals and direct them toward your performance, not the result of your performance. In other words, make it your goal to shoot each shot with the best form possible. Remember, a perfect shot is nothing more than a perfect shot execution.

When shooting an arrow, the mind and body must work together as one unit. This unit becomes the shot. As you participate in a tournament, you are standing there for one reason, to shoot the arrow. Nothing else should enter into the picture. Shooting the arrow is the event and that is the focus. You must free yourself from other thoughts, relax, and enjoy the moment. Become absorbed in the experience and think in the present. Do not reflect on the past or the future. Do not think about the last shot or the outcome of the present shot. Focus on the moment, trusting your mind and body to execute that perfect shot which you have practiced. Having a top performance will take care of itself.

Raise Your Level of Concentration

Earlier in my career, while shooting a state indoor championship, I let my bow down five or six times. The pin just would not settle in on the "dot." With a minute left on the clock, I was the last person on the line when I shot. The arrow hit its mark and the line judge blew the whistle.

"Hold it!" I'm not done!" I exclaimed. The next shot went much easier and the arrow slammed into the center with 30 seconds remaining. The whistle sounded again.

"Hold it! I still have one left," I said.

By now, everyone was watching, and the place became very quiet. I kept telling myself, "Concentrate and shoot good form." I then executed another sound shot.

When we went to pull arrows another archer inquired, "How can you concentrate after all of those interruptions?"

My reply was, "I concentrate really hard because the shot is very important to me. If someone offers you a thousand dollars to thread a needle on the very first try, how hard would you concentrate?"

"Really hard," he replied.

This type of mental approach is what you should be using on each shot in a tournament. You have to stay focused on the task that is in front of you. Concentrate and make the best shot that you are capable of producing. Develop the attitude, "I will thread the needle."

Archery is a sport of concentration and steady nerves. Focused mental thinking will help eliminate or reduce tournament anxiety. Top archers are not born with this gift; they develop and fine-tune it over the years. Because concentration is learned on the practice field and refined and mastered on the tournament field, it is important to participate in as many competitions as possible. Once each shoot is over, work to analyze and evaluate your performance. If you got nervous or lost your concentration, try to identify the reason so it can be corrected. Make every tournament a learning experience in that, whether you win or lose, you can look for ways to improve.

While you develop these abilities on the practice field, do not expect to walk onto the tournament field and just have them. Try to hone these skills by shooting every practice shot with the same degree of intensity as you would if you were competing in a national championship. Each individual practice shot should be treated as the most important shot you are going to execute that day. If you are at full draw and the pin will not "steady up" or if you have negative thoughts and are not staying focused, do not release the arrow. Stop! Keep your focal point on your shooting process and then re-address the target.

When practicing alone, it helps give the experience meaning. Try testing different pieces of equipment such as arrows, rests, stabilizers, etc. You will be forced to concentrate as you attempt to get more valid testing results. Do not hesitate to also make minor changes with your present equipment. Then, while you re-sight the bow, limit yourself to three shots at each distance, which increases your mental focus. As you practice with bullseye targets, keep score to measure your performance and enhance concentration. Most archers put far too much emphasis on their points during a tournament and ignore them during practice. Instead, raise the importance of each arrow shot during drill and lower the value of each arrow in a tournament. With effort, the gap between the two should narrow. Before you can master holding your focus when shooting before a crowd, you have to develop it while practicing at home.

Once concentration is learned under calm, ideal conditions, start adding a few distractions to your practice routine. Attach a piece of paper to a stick and allow it to blow back and forth around the bullseye. Train during a strong, gusty wind or light rain. Try placing a radio beside you and tune it to a talk show. Better yet, invite that friend that "won't quit talking" over to practice with you. When you are handling these distractions well, join some friends to shoot targets for score. Make your own rules that create distractions, such as talking and harassing the opponent, as long as you do not touch the person or create a dangerous situation. Shoot ten shots with each game while keeping score. Wagering is optional, but is a good way to add more pressure. It is a fun competition that will truly test your concentration.

Participate in as many tournaments as you are able without getting burned out. Attend different kinds of events, such as 3-D, field, and indoor target. Each will help as you develop into a well-rounded, accomplished archer.

Build a Positive Self-Image

In the 1990s, sixteen-year-old Ashley Kamuf made the U.S. Indoor Team for the World Championship to be held in Cuba. She had to compete against the top women archers from forty-five countries. I managed to get a description of the interior of the building where the competition was to be held. As a regular part of her practice routine, every night she would sit in a chair, stare at a target and mentally shoot the tournament. She knew part of the crowd would be chanting, "USA! USA!" Using imagery, her feelings and thoughts were saying, "This is fun and my friends are supporting me." There were two large scoreboards on the wall with the names and running scores for her and her competitor. She would visualize this and think, "That looks cool, but I don't need to worry about the points until the match is over." She would visualize a TV camera fifteen feet behind her and she would think, "Good. Now everyone can see what good form I shoot."

When the World Championship was completed and the gold medal had been awarded, Ashley called me and exclaimed, "I won!"

During our conversation, I asked, "Were you nervous?"

Her reply was, “Not really. I am more nervous now with all of the attention. The matches were fun and just like what I had practiced every night.”

Mental training will build a positive self-image. Picturing yourself shooting every arrow with perfect form will enhance your form, raise your level of focus, and give you a positive picture of your ability to perform. When an archer walks to the line and thinks, “I don’t want to embarrass myself,” the chances for effective results decrease rapidly. If an archer approaches the line and mentally says, “I can shoot this shot with perfect form,” then a successful shot is more likely to follow.

The development of self-image should be focused on your ability to perform and not as the result of the performance. You should picture and feel yourself shooting the perfect shot. You can control your capacity to perform and shoot an excellent shot. You cannot control whether you win because that is based on the skill of others as well as yourself. Sometimes the luck of a line call can make the difference. I always have maintained that there are more tournaments lost than there are won. Many archers have the potential to win the tournaments; instead, they let the pressure overcome them and lose the competitions. True, the titles of some tournaments are captured with a fantastic score. However, most events are won with a finish that many of the contenders are capable of achieving. If these archers had thought positively about their ability to shoot and execute a good shot, perhaps they would have stood in the winner’s circle.

A positive self-image helps reduce nervousness and anxiety because you can place yourself in a comfort zone. If you feel confident that you can execute a good shot, then your mind will not be directed at negative scenarios.

During mental practice, try to simulate the upcoming tournament conditions. See and feel yourself executing every shot to the best of your ability. Be aware of the excitement surrounding the event. Look at it and appreciate it for what it is, an opportunity for you to enjoy your sport and prove that you can shoot every shot with perfect form. Isn't that what you have been doing in practice? We train so we can reproduce the same shot every time. When the tournament is at hand, place your confidence where it belongs, and that is in your ability to duplicate the shot.

Chapter 6. Practice

Video Your Shot

All archers would like to improve their shooting skills. Some can afford the luxury of a private coach or attend a good shooters' school, while others cannot. Any person can become a good archer with or without a coach, but the advantage of having a coach is to shorten the learning curve and to get you back on track quickly when you encounter trouble. The whole key to becoming a good shot is consistency. There isn't necessarily a right way or a wrong way to shoot, although the use of certain muscle groups when executing a shot can make it much easier to develop consistency. When I work with an archer, I am looking for discrepancies in his or her form. If the person is doing something in a different way than the mental picture I have of perfect form, I do not worry about it as long as the individual does it the same every time. This is what you need to observe and evaluate in your own form.

To review, the archery shot is actually relatively simple. The bow arm needs to have consistent pressure towards the target and the release arm needs to maintain consistent pressure away from the target. First, consider the bow arm. The forward pressure should be executed with the same amount of force and in the same direction on every shot. Examine your form by shooting numerous shots at a bullseye target at 10 yards. Pay attention to how your bow arm reacts. If done properly, it should move to the same position each time the arrow is released. Once you have mastered this, shoot the target at twenty yards for score. Set up a video camera in front of you and film a shooting series. Afterwards, evaluate the reaction of your bow arm to see if you maintained consistency. A common problem that occurs is when an archer attempts to over-aim the shot. When this happens, the degree and angle of forward pressure is changed and the bow arm reacts differently. Because the majority of the misses come from the bow arm, include strong concentration and form work in your training routine.

Next, look at the release arm and hand. Shoot a series of shots from ten yards at a bullseye target and video the process. When viewing the tape, examine it to determine if your release hand took the same path and ended in the same position on each shot. If not, continue shooting at 10 yards until you achieve consistency. If you are trying to maintain back pressure with your arm muscles, it will be difficult to be consistent. The process is much easier if you pull with the muscles in your back. Once you have established a good release at ten yards, shoot at 20 yards for score. Again, video and evaluate the sequence. A benefit of recording your shots is having the proof that your form is consistent. If you are not replicating your shots, you can identify where you are having difficulty.

After you have cleaned up both the bow arm and the release arm, it is time to evaluate the whole shot process. Shoot, score, and video a series of 20 shots at the same target, but this time move back to thirty yards. Following each shot, call out the score of the arrow in order to have it recorded on video. At the longer distance, it is common for an archer to over-aim the shot in an attempt to fine-tune the sight pin. When this occurs, the shooting rhythm slows and the form starts breaking down. Go over the video and identify where your form changed on any missed shots. Once you have identified the problem, you will be able to correct it. By becoming more involved in the shot process and examining it through video, you can develop a more consistent form and successfully shoot tighter groups.

Better Focus for Better Performance

Sometimes when you are shooting, every arrow goes in the middle. It seems effortless and you can do no wrong. You are in what many people call the "zone." For a large number of archers, this occurrence is far too rare. Why is it that sometimes it seems almost impossible to miss the bullseye and on other occasions it seems like you are shooting at a moving target? A poor performance often occurs because you are bombarding your mind with negative thoughts and apprehensions about what might happen. You are being concerned with things that have nothing to do with the execution of your shots, such as too much attention on score or winning. Winning is the result of a good performance. The only way an archer can have a top game is by staying relaxed and focused on a positive shot process.

The legendary Tom Amberry worked with professional basketball players and taught them how to shoot free throws (Amberry). His credentials as a free throw shooter speak for themselves, showing he once produced 2,750 consecutive free throws. Even at age 80, he commonly made 500 in a row. He maintained the most common error of free throw shooters is that they are thinking about sinking a basket. Instead, he shifted their focus toward the process of achieving the perfect shot. He taught them to become mentally absorbed in a positive picture of their shooting routine. By doing this, they freed their minds of the negative thinking that produced apprehension and anxiety. Making a free throw is no different from shooting an arrow. Both need to be executed with a relaxed, rhythmic sequence.

The majority of the Olympic athletes use mental training to enhance their performance. The mental routine differs among athletes, but the common factor used by nearly all of them is a positive picture of the act of their performance. This produces a controlled state of security and calmness, which allows the athlete to create his or her "zone" in which to perform.

Why is it that so many archers do so well on the practice range and have difficulties on the tournament field? In competition, they cannot stay relaxed, but instead misdirect their point of focus. Create your own "zone" for your performance. Mentally picture yourself shooting the perfect shot. See the arrow hitting the mark. At a tournament, continually fill your thinking with these positive images and there will be no room for the intrusive negative thoughts to emerge.

If you make a bad shot, do not dwell on it. Instead, picture yourself making several perfect hits. If you shoot a lot of perfect shots in a row, forget them. Begin forming a mental image of the best form that you can use on your next shot. Too many consecutive good shots can be just as detrimental as a poor one, for if you dwell on them, your point of focus can easily shift to winning. The result will be anxiety, which can cause your form to suffer. You should only focus on the next arrow that you have to shoot. You get to the top of an icy stairway by taking one deliberate step at a time. If you focus on the top of the staircase or the last step where you had trouble, you can easily fall. Focus and live in the moment. This mindset will enhance your chances for success, whether climbing the icy stairs or shooting a sixty-arrow tournament.

Some of my most accomplished archers have told me that they are mentally drained at the end of a tournament. By keeping their attention on shooting perfect form, they had a peak performance, though they were exhausted at the end. If tournament pressure seems to hurt you in competition, try raising your degree of focus. Before you shoot and during your shot sequence, concentrate on the best form you can produce. This heightened level of positive focus should help you have a top performance.

Make Practice and Tournament Scores the Same

In his youth, Ryan Day had been shooting archery for only five months, but there he was competing in the NFAA Indoor National Target Championship in the cub division. During the tournament, I would periodically stop by and inquire, "Are you running your mental program and shooting perfect form?"

"Yes, I'm doing everything the same as I do in practice," he would reply. When the tournament was over, Ryan had shot a 600 with 118 X's and had set a new national record.

At the conclusion of the tournament, some archers were very pleased with their performance, but many were upset. Why were they dissatisfied? Think of the last time you were frustrated after finishing a competition. Was it because you did not win? It probably was not. You were disappointed because you knew that you had the ability to shoot a better game than you did. Your tournament scores fell well short of your practice scores.

Winning a tournament is nothing more than putting extra icing on a cake. The real winning is for the archer to shoot the best possible tournament that he or she is capable of achieving. I like the way our son Vic, a three-time Olympian, responded to a reporter after a gold medal match at the Olympics. The reporter asked, "How does it feel to lose the gold medal?" Vic replied, "I didn't lose the gold. I shot good and won the silver. He shot better and won the gold."

A true champion can take the same scores from the practice range and reproduce them on the tournament field. Sometimes you may win when performing poorly. Another time you may shoot great and lose because someone shot better. The most important thing is that you execute the best shots you can possibly produce. If that score is not high enough to take home a trophy and that is what you want, then you need to raise the degree of your skill. Increasing your practice time or concentration level might do this for you. However, if you feel that you have reached a plateau and are not going forward, then seek help from a professional coach.

You have to be a good shot to win tournaments. Good form and consistent shot execution are a must. This is learned on the practice field while shooting at blank bales and bullseye targets. No matter how great a shot you are, it will not yield success if you cannot duplicate that shot on the tournament field. Why is it that many people who are excellent archers have trouble taking their skills from the practice level to the competition level? The two main obstacles preventing this transfer are anxiety and loss of concentration. Anxiety is probably the biggest culprit in causing most archers to perform below their potential. They start thinking about the tournament in terms of, "I hope I can win," "I have to beat my buddy or I will never hear the end of it," "What will people think if I don't do well?" or "I know I cannot drop any points if I want to win."

Once a series of these unproductive thoughts start, they quickly engulf the thinking process and an archer cannot concentrate on shooting good form. Such anxiety also produces tense muscles. This is why I stress the importance of a relaxed, trouble-free form. An archer must stay relaxed in order to shoot effective form. So how do you stop anxiety from growing like a "wildfire?" You do it the same way that you would handle any unwanted crisis. First, try to not let it get started. Secondly, if it does begin, get it stopped quickly. Anxiety is caused by what you are thinking; therefore, stop any harmful ideas from entering your mind! Your brain cannot concentrate on two thought patterns at once, so replace those anxious ideas with images of you shooting a perfect shot. The first few times you try this thought replacement, you will discover that it helps some. The more that you use it and incorporate it into your archery program, the more you will be able to relax and focus on shooting with good form.

Concentration is nothing more than the thought process staying directed at executing a perfect shot. It sounds very simple and it is ... as long as you do not allow other ideas to enter into your mind. How do some archers shoot the highest scores of their lives in the big tournaments? Each shot is very important, so they concentrate harder to make each one with the best form that they can muster. The archers that I coach have set or broken over 450 national and world records. Most of these records were the highest scores they had ever produced, including practice scores. They concentrated and made sure every shot was with precise form. This is why it is vital for you to shoot every practice shot the same way as you would in a tournament. Then, when you are in a competition, remember to execute every shot the same as you do on the practice field. Staying disciplined and following this mental program will make you a winner because you will be performing to the best of your ability.

Mental Imaging

Years ago, one of my top students had an exciting and busy summer of activities. She had not picked up her bow in nearly a month and was heading off to a national championship. Trying to make the best of the situation, I advised her to shoot hundreds of arrows a day with her visualization program. When she got to the tournament, she was to use the practice day for blank bale shooting to get her form perfected. At the conclusion of the tournament she called, with excitement in her voice, "I did it. I won! I shot my highest score in my match against the world champion!"

A strong mental program can help an archer perform at top level. Note, I said help. I do not recommend using it to replace good hard practice, but if that is your only option, use it. Imaging works best when it is combined with strong physical practice, which is needed to give you muscle memory and to build stamina.

To learn imagery programming, I recommend sitting back in a comfortable easy chair. Close your eyes and mentally go through each step of shooting an arrow, following the same arrow sequence that you would use if you were actually making a shot. The first several times you perform this, actually hold your arms out and go through the motions. As the image becomes clearer, stop raising your arms physically and do the whole shot process in your mind. See the mental image from the viewpoint of you, the archer, making the shot. Feel yourself performing the sequence. Make it as real as possible as you feel the muscles required to pull and hold the bow, see the sight pin settle in on the target, hear the bow go off, experience the recoil, see the bow arm finish straight at the target, and see your nock appear in the 10 ring.

The more you can feel and see, the more vivid the process will become. The more relaxed you are, the more real the experience will be. As the mental process grows stronger, the image that is left in your mind will help you build good form and confidence.

The whole process will grow and develop as you practice it. Eventually, you will be able to use the method at any time and in any place. I have been in shoot-offs in front of hundreds of people. Once I start running my mental program, there is no one there but me and the target. My whole focus is on shooting a shot with perfect form. The degree to which you can program your thinking and mind will be regulated by your ability to concentrate and practice mental imagery.

Mental imaging, like shooting a bow, does not come in one or two practice sessions. It continues to grow and become stronger each time you use it. One year I was giving so many archery lessons that I didn't have enough time for my own shooting practice. In the evenings I would go downstairs to our archery room and shoot at a blank bale for about half an hour. To my surprise, when I would go to an indoor target tournament, I found I was shooting some of the best indoor scores that I had ever accomplished. Why? By repeatedly reinforcing the steps of good form with the people I was helping, I engraved the image of good form in my mind. Working with my students had also strengthened my own shooting.

Imaging is a very useful tool in correcting a flaw in your form. For example, if you are collapsing and not consistently applying pressure to the string with the release arm, run your mental program repeatedly, while picturing yourself applying good pressure. Then go in front of the target, close your eyes, and actually shoot the shot as you visualize it. This method allows you to address the problem without being overly concerned with the other aspects of the shot process. Keep practicing with the blank bale until the correct back pressure is incorporated into your shooting sequence.

Mental imagery used in conjunction with blank bale shooting is one of the best methods for correcting a flaw in shooting form, as well as giving your muscles and mind the memory needed to execute a perfect shot. It leaves your mind with a positive picture of your form and your ability to produce your best shot. Skilled mental imaging fosters confidence, which in turn produces success.

Using Positive Mental Training Techniques

One of my students was in the shoot-down round at an ASA tournament. He went to the stake, set his sight, attached his release, and stood motionless staring at the target for nearly a minute. I knew the shot that was soon to follow would be perfect; and it was. This archer had prepared himself mentally to execute a shot with perfect form.

If an archer develops a picture of the perfect shot, he or she can enhance his or her performance in a tournament. It should be both a positive picture and a feeling of the best shot possible. To develop and strengthen your mental imagery and feeling of the perfect shot, make it a part of your routine to go to the practice range and shoot a blank bale with your eyes closed. Relax your body and practice shooting perfect form. Feel the muscles involved and the explosion of the shot. When you are comfortable with this feeling, try to duplicate it without the bow in your hand. Shoot the shot exactly the same as you did when the bow was a part of the process. Next, lower your arms and shoot the same shot mentally without arm movement. You should be able to feel the muscles and the shot execution even though you are not physically moving.

Finally, shoot the same shot, both physically and mentally, at a target. When the shot feels perfect and the arrow goes into the mark, proceed to close your eyes and repeat the process several times in your mind. Feel the shot and see the arrow hitting the mark. This repeated exercise will give you the perfect picture and feeling for your mental imagery training. You will experience the form that you want in your mental training, as you develop it in practice and at tournaments. Making mental imagery a regular part of your regimen will give you confidence, ingrain your best shot into your thinking, and carry over into your performance.

Mental training is a valuable tool for archers as well as athletes in any sport; and most Olympic athletes use some form of mental training. In archery it plays a very significant role because precise muscle movement and calm concentration regulate archery performance. The use of mental imagery can enhance both of these attributes.

Laura Wilkinson, an Olympic diver, broke her foot in several places and could not physically practice for the Olympic tryouts. She did, however, practice her daily diving exercises with mental imagery. A couple of weeks before the tryouts, she started walking and won her position on the United States Olympic Team. I watched as she stood on the diving platform performing her mental imagery before each dive. Her walking was hampered by her injury, but her performance was not. She went on to capture the gold medal in Sydney, Australia.

As noted earlier, mental training prepares the body both

mentally and physically. An archer practices it so the shot can be repeated exactly the same. Even though we think of this process as conditioning the mind, it also trains the muscles and nerves used to execute the shot. We are actually blueprinting the perfect shot in our mind and muscles. When the arrow is set and released in mental training, the same muscles needed to perform the actual shot are affected. The mind sends impulses to those muscles, which in turn programs them for the shot execution. You need to develop trust in your ability to duplicate the shot and not in your ability to score. Score is the result of using good form. Repeated mental practice makes the shot become more routine, natural, and fluid. The confidence that results allows the archer to perform with ease when faced with a variety of situations and unexpected circumstances.

There are different levels of mental practice, with visualization serving as one part of the process. In visualization, you will see yourself shooting the arrow, just as if you were making the actual shot. You will view the situation while looking outward, rather than from the point of another observer.

Mental imagery is a higher level of mental training and takes longer to master. You are still visualizing the shot, but now you must become actively involved in the experience with your other senses. You are actually creating the complete shot scenario in your mind. You feel the back pressure, the explosion of the shot and the reaction of your bow arm. By seeing and feeling the perfect shot, you can program both the muscles and the mind so the execution can be duplicated under a pressure situation.

Mental imagery is very effective because with practice our muscles actually contract and respond in the same manner as if the bow were in our hands. The only difference is that one will experience very little physical movement. It is essential that you picture the perfect shot with the same rhythm as you normally use because the result will be the shot that you are programming into your mind and muscles. This level of mental practice raises your power of concentration and focus.

Imagery will also help an archer control anxiety, nervousness and muscle tension. The mind can create the tense atmosphere of a world championship. Think of yourself facing some of the most difficult shooting circumstances possible; then, view yourself remaining calm and shooting the perfect shot. Mental imagery will affirm your ability to shoot effectively. Picture yourself in a positive manner and you will have the confidence to perform in a positive manner.

Chapter 7. Putting It All Together

Get Ready for the Nationals

As the first day of an Indoor National Tournament drew to a close, a fellow archer could not conceal his frustration and embarrassment. For the past three years, his worst performance in an indoor round had been a 57X, with his average scores hovering around the 59-60X range. Feeling ready to tackle the national level, the gentleman was mentally unprepared for the 298, 52X he saw on his initial score card. He had reason to be upset. The mighty power of competition pressure had thrown my friend into a tailspin, though I'm quite sure he was not the only archer in the arena who was experiencing the dreaded phenomena of bullseye shrinkage, where the 10 ring looked like an aspirin.

The only way to get use to coping with pressure is to subject yourself to it frequently and to learn to repress it mentally. If you do the majority of your practices in calm surroundings, you will find it very difficult to perform well at the national level, when hundreds of people are around you and you think you have to hit the X ring. Begin looking for opportunities requiring you to perform under stress. When you go to the local range, select a lane where others will see you and everything you do. Have you noticed there are often open lanes near the entry where people frequently stop and observe the archers? Select one of these and practice ignoring the commotion and spectators as you shoot your game.

To simulate shooting under pressure, try getting together with some friends who shoot close to your level of performance. Make a game of putting a dollar into a pot for each 10 arrows shot, eventually awarding the money to the person with the highest score. Before long you will grow accustom to the pressure, improve your focus, and enjoy the experience. If not, make sure you bring a lot of dollar bills!

You can also simulate the start of the national championship. Have people shoot right next to you on both sides. Mentally "work yourself up" and make yourself nervous by acting as if this really were the first day of the competition. Then shoot for score. Sometimes pretend you have a great score going, the next arrows are your last 5 shots, and they have to be in. Calm yourself mentally and then use good form. Try to make the practice as if it were a tournament and then try to make the tournament as if it were the practice.

Another method when playing in league is to tell a family member that if you do not shoot a certain score, you will do the household chores the next day. Now, most of you who are familiar with my coaching know that I do not want archers to put emphasis on score. I still do not, but points are a part of the game. You know you have to shoot a certain score in order to place. During competition, do not worry about the numbers; worry about shooting the best form you can execute. You can always think about the score when you are done with the tournament.

Finally, to be successful under pressure, learn mental imagery and practice it daily. Use it not only in archery, but also incorporate it into your daily living. The art of practicing mental control will make you an accomplished archer, a better worker, and a stronger person. Most of all, remember that archery is a sport to be enjoyed. Lighten up and make sure you are having a great time!

Been There – Done That

The wind was blowing about 15 mph and it was raining. Our daughter Sally turned to me and remarked, "I think it's time to go outside and practice." For the next couple of hours, we shot in the rain and wind. Practicing under these conditions has paid dividends on numerous occasions, as we have competed at many tournaments where rain was inevitable. If an archer has practiced in inclement weather and learned how to handle the challenges associated with it, then that person will be able to confront those conditions with confidence and greater success.

When you are facing a difficult shot in a tournament and your mind says, "Been there – done that," then you can address the competitive situation with poise. Practice is not just about shooting arrows; it is the time that you must prepare yourself mentally as well as physically. Place top priority on every arrow, treating each as the most important one you will shoot that day. I am sure most archers put a high value on every arrow executed on a 40-target course. Use that same emphasis with each practice shot, and then you will feel more comfortable mentally when shooting in a tournament.

For an exercise, select one shot and designate it as a sudden death shoot-off. Try to create tension and pressure in your mind and then practice focusing your concentration on making the shot. You must rehearse shooting under pressure or you will not know how to handle anxiety during a tournament. Compete against yourself in 10-arrow tournaments on bullseye targets. Record your scores and try to beat yourself each following round. The exercise will give each arrow more importance than routinely shooting at the target.

Choose times to practice when you are tired. If you are exhausted from doing manual work, try shooting your bow for score. Maybe you just completed a long, hard, 40-target course. Go to the practice range and see what effects this has on your shooting. Knowing the outcome is very important because many tournaments are lost during the last 10 targets on a long course. Any problem can be corrected, as long as you identify the difficulty.

Using a commercial archery log or notebook, keep accurate records of each shot taken during a tournament. Study the data you collect and note if a pattern develops. For example, I personally shoot a little left on the first two targets and then settle into my normal shot for the remainder of the game. Knowing this, I adjust the sights for the first few targets to compensate for it. You may find that you shoot to the right on downhill or uphill shots. Whatever the case may be, you will be able to identify the problem and then take the proper measures to correct it.

When practicing for a competition, try to simulate as many of the tournament conditions as possible. Put primary emphasis on any situations that cause you difficulty. On one occasion, low-light surroundings in dark woods were giving me challenges. Too big an aperture for bright sunlight was making it difficult to shoot a tight group. The problem was solved by installing a peep with an adjustable aperture.

If you find you are distracted easily, create unnecessary commotion when you are practicing. Shoot with a friend and ask him to safely disrupt your shooting. If performing in wind is the problem, then train when the wind is blowing. Whatever dilemma you face in tournament situations, your mind should be able to confidently say, "Been there – done that."

Take Two Practice Shots at the First Target

One of my top-level students was getting ready to go to the first line at an indoor national target championship when I asked him, "Are you focused?"

"Yes, but I'm still a little nervous," he replied.

"That's no problem. Just take two practice shots at the first target and you'll be ready," I suggested.

That is just what he did. When he released the third arrow at the first bullseye, it went into the X ring.

At this point you are probably thinking, "That is against the rules," or perhaps, "Wouldn't it be nice to take a couple practice shots before I shoot the one that counts?"

Actually, you can take two legal practice shots. Stand at the line, load your bow, and visualize yourself shooting perfect form while hitting the X ring. The third time, shoot the same shot, both physically and mentally. The image of the first two shots will calm you and create a positive picture in your mind. The third arrow will then be very easy because in your mind you have already made two successful hits at the X ring.

Mental imagery is nearly as effective as executing the actual shot (see **Mental Imaging** pg. 108). The trick is to practice daily until your thinking becomes a part of the process, as you see and feel the shot execution without having to physically move your muscles. It takes work and focus to allow your mind and body to become more involved in the event. When you see your groups tighten and your form become more consistent, include in your training a less subdued setting, such as rehearsing in front of the television or in a crowded room. This technique will raise the level of your performance in a competition because you are increasing the degree and intensity of your concentration.

Mastering mental imagery will allow you to bring your thought process into focus almost instantly. When your thinking is totally involved in the shot, external stimuli such as pressure and crowds will not be as strong of an influence. You will discover that duplicating those shots perfected during practice will come more naturally in a tournament setting and you can enjoy taking those two extra practice shots at the first target.

Stay in Rhythm

The final shots were fired and score cards were totaled at an indoor national championship. Hunter Tuveson of the young adult division found himself tied with 118X. Minutes clicked by while we waited for the opportunity to determine the winner. My advice to Hunter was simple: "Before the shoot-off, run your mental program so you will be ready. During the practice ends, be aggressive and establish your rhythm. Shoot the scoring ends the same way." The young man made all of his shots like a programmed machine, as he walked away with the national title.

Successful archers maintain a closely-timed, rhythmic shot sequence, which is an essential element in producing tight arrow groups. Then why does an archer change his or her rhythm during a tournament? Why does it seem easier to shoot a strong, aggressive shot during practice than it does in competition? To find the answers to these questions, look at an archer's objective and attitude.

During practice, the main emphasis is normally on making a shot with good form. You are relaxed, so there is very little sight movement and the shot seems much easier. In a tournament, however, one's thinking often shifts from proper shot execution to that of hitting the bullseye or capturing the winner's trophy. The added pressure builds anxiety and produces tension that causes excessive sight movement. What is the best way you can overcome this problem? First, try to keep your thinking focused on creating a perfect shot and not on the result of where the arrow might hit. In an important tournament, most archers encounter more sight movement than they do during practice. The difference between the winners and the losers is how well they control this stress and strive to carry out a strong shot. When unnecessary seconds are added to your normal sequence, as you wait for the pin to be in that perfect spot, your back pressure begins to decrease and a poor shot execution is inevitable. Instead, you have to learn the process of trusting your form and shooting a strong, aggressive shot.

If you realize that you are more nervous than you can comfortably handle, let the bow down. Take several seconds of slow, deep breathing and concentrate on relaxing the muscles in your neck and shoulders. Accept the fact that you are going to see more sight movement. Then draw the bow, trust your form, and follow through with the completion of the shot. When you do, it will be the best shot you are capable of making under those circumstances.

In a tournament, there are often two typical times that an archer becomes more nervous. One happens during the first two targets because most archers want to start the competition on a positive note and have built up apprehension about how well they are going to perform. To alleviate this potential difficulty, try to simulate excessive pin movement during practice so you can be more comfortable in a tournament situation. Try running for a while to raise your pulse rate. Then pick up your bow and pretend that the target you are shooting is the first one of an important competition. Yes, you will see more pin movement, but you are going to have to trust your form and make a strong shot.

If you are fortunate, there will be a second opportunity to experience extra tension. This happens after you have been shooting successfully and begin to realize that you are in a position to win. Your attitude shifts from producing excellent form to that of winning, so you become more anxious. Such thinking needs to be reversed immediately. In your mind, begin replaying all of the good shots that you have been making. Then, picture yourself repeating these on the target in front of you. Be aggressive and go for that strong shot. If you have the same routine as you did with the successful shots, you may just find yourself in the winner's circle.

Confidence and the Positive Approach

Approaching a target at a 3-D tournament, one of the archers in my group remarked, "This is a difficult shot." It was a small deer at 40 yards. My turn came first and I made a successful hit.

The shooter following me in the rotation stepped up to the stake, looked at the target, and then turned back to me. "Weren't you worried about that tree?" he asked.

"What tree?" I responded. "There isn't a tree in front of the 10 ring."

Actually, there was a small two inch sapling standing in front of the target, just in line with the center of the 8 ring. The fact that there was a tree blocking part of the scoring area never entered my mind as I made that shot. It wasn't obstructing the 10 ring, and that was my only focus.

This type of shot is common at local 3-D tournaments. An archer simply cannot permit a tree or hindrance to distract him or her from the shooting process. Many hunting shots are made with obstructions near the shooting lane. A person must have confidence and concentrate strictly on the center of the kill zone. If the tree were not there, most archers would have considered that particular shot to be comparatively easy. So, ignore the tree, believe in yourself, and make the shot!

Confidence is an important factor when it comes to tournament shooting. You must truly believe that you can "10 ring" the target, no matter how small or how far away it is. This does not guarantee that you will always hit the 10, but it means that you will feel capable of capturing the bullseye. How does an archer achieve this kind of confidence? Diligent effort! Strive to practice and learn to make every type of shot that you may confront on a 3-D course. Then, when faced with a challenging shot in a competition, you will truly believe you can score because you have already proven it to yourself many times.

A top archer will identify any weakness he or she has and then work to make this a strength. As you participate in events throughout the year, keep track of targets, settings, distances, and conditions that give you trouble. Any weakness, including the wind, distance to the target, difficult footing conditions, or poor lighting, can be practiced and mastered. If you have not overcome these challenges, then you will not have the confidence to successfully conquer them in competition. Once the more difficult shots are learned, the average ones will be easier to perform.

Cub, youth, and women archers can work on the difficult shots by shooting all of their local tournaments from the adult men's stakes. At a national level, the shots they encounter will typically be more demanding than those offered at the smaller competitions. If an archer treats the local tournaments as practice and learns to shoot the challenging shots, then the ones at the national level will seem less demanding. I used this technique with my own children. When they were in the cub division, they commented that the targets at the national and world championships were much easier than what they were accustomed to shooting at the local events. They definitely had more confidence when they addressed the targets at the more advance competitions.

The serious shooter can learn a great deal spending an afternoon with a portable target in a rolling section of woods. Practice shooting uphill, downhill, side hill, and from hill-to-hill across gullies. When you find a target setting that is giving you trouble, go to work on it. After learning how to consistently make the shot, you will have the confidence necessary to make similar shots at a tournament.

Above all, be honest and realistic with yourself. If you encounter a 40-yard turkey, you know that the small 10 ring on this target would be difficult enough to hit, even if you knew the exact yardage. You should be confident the arrow will hold the 8 ring and recognize that it will require a perfect shot for a 10. Then ready your bow and concentrate on a making a perfect shot.

If you are scoring 80% "10's" in practice, then you cannot expect better than that at a tournament. The 20% that are not "10's" are going to show up somewhere during the shoot. Realize and accept it, and try to score as high as your capabilities will allow. If you want to score higher, then you must accept the fact that you will need to work on your game to raise your potential. With confidence, concentration, and effort you can elevate your achievement to a higher level.

An archer should develop the confidence that he or she can make every shot on the course. You should also realize that it is difficult to do everything perfect on 40 targets. When shooting in a tournament, your goal should not be to win the event. Instead, it should be to shoot perfect form on each of the 40 targets. You should have 40 goals. Forget each target after it has been scored and go to the next goal - the target! Confidence and concentration will produce higher scores and high scores make winners.

Stay Focused

During a 3-D competition, I was observing a group of archers who were just finishing the course. As they were hanging up their gear on the rack near me, they were joined by a buddy.

"How did you do?" the friend asked.

"I should have done a lot better," he responded.

Another said, "I missed a couple of easy shots. Other than that, I did great."

How many times have you heard comments like these or perhaps made them yourself? Contrary to popular opinion, most bad scores in 3-D tournaments are not because of problems in judging the distance to the target. The troublesome scores are often caused by an archer who did not stay focused during the shot. True, he or she might have been a little off on the yardage, but the problem was exaggerated when anxiety crept into the game. Concentration and positive thinking are key elements in achieving high scores.

Based on my experience, only 5% of all archers can shoot as well in a tournament as in practice. And interestingly, 2% of all archers will actually shoot better in a tournament than in practice. Why do most archers fail to shoot as well in a tournament, yet a small number actually achieve better? Their mental approach and concentration level during each shot are the deciding factors.

Archery is a precision-type sport that requires deep concentration, much the same as golf, basketball, or tennis. Picture yourself coaching a basketball team and the score is tied with 10 seconds remaining. Your superstar guard is having a so-so game and the forward has been carrying the team all night. With ten seconds remaining and one chance to score and win the game, your forward pleads, "Give me the ball and I'll make it." Which player do you want to take the last shot?

When you walk up to the shooting stake on the 3-D course and see a javelina over 40 yards away, what goes through your mind? Do you confide to yourself, "That's too great a distance for me to hit a target that size, though I'd sure like it to happen."

If this is what you think, I can almost guarantee the little piggy will go "wee-wee-wee… all the way home." Mentally, you are not going to be able to concentrate on the shot. Your negative thinking will be a stronger influence than your thoughts of making a good shot with proper form. With a pessimistic attitude controlling your muscles and reflexes, you will likely miss the shot.

If, however, you look at the javelina and honestly think that you will bring home the bacon, the odds are now in your favor. A good 3-D shooter believes and expects to "10" every target on the course.

One of the cardinal rules of winning is as follows: *When you don't think you are going to make the shot, don't shoot*. It's as simple as that. Let down your bow, refocus your thoughts, and take a positive approach to the shot.

I was competing in an important tournament, letting down on one target three times. With the fourth attempt, I executed the shot and captured a 10. One of the fellows in the group stopped me and asked, "How do you force yourself to let down?"

"I have only one shot at each target," I explained, "so it has to be the best that I have to offer. I will not shoot if I don't think it is going to be a 10."

"I understand that, but I still can't make myself let down," he lamented.

"Do you let down in practice'?" I asked.

He replied, "No. It is easier to just shoot the arrow."

"And, isn't that what is happening now?"

It's imperative that you make practice conditions as close to an actual tournament as possible. I've stressed so often that concentration and discipline are learned on the practice field and practiced on the tournament field. If this sounds strange, you must remember there are few distractions in a practice setting. The only place to really test your mental control is at a competition or by performing pressure situation where people are watching.

Many times an archer's biggest enemy is his or her own ego. To become a champion, you must learn to concentrate on your next shot. Forget about anyone else's score, even your own. Shoot each tournament one arrow at a time. If it goes in the 10 ring, pat yourself on the back and savor the moment. If you miss, you may take a moment to mentally reprimand yourself; but as soon as the score is recorded, forget it. Whatever it is – put it behind you. Go on and prepare for the next target.

Champions understand that to win a tournament they must first conquer themselves. Actually, the only person who can beat you is yourself. Accept the fact that you are going to make good shots and bad shots. Some days the 10 ring seems to be the size of an aspirin and every shot is a struggle. Other days it is the size of a washtub and you can't miss. With either situation, let each shot be the best you have to offer. Many times you will find that your highest scores come on one of the struggling days. Know that any archer can score when he is shooting well. Only a good archer can score when he is having trouble. The difference is staying focused.

Believe in Yourself

About an hour before the gold medal matches of a Junior World Championship in Sweden, I received two phone calls. One was from a young man and the other was from a young lady, both of whom were shooting for the gold. Each of these youth were 15 years old and were competing against peers as old as age 18. Despite their ages, they were emotionally very mature. My conversation with each archer was quite similar:

"You can shoot every shot with the very same form and you have proven that thousands of times in practice. You have a strong mental program. Make sure you run it with every shot. Believe in yourself and your ability to shoot the same shot. Do not be concerned with score or winning. It will take care of itself. Shoot perfect form with good rhythm and you will do the best that you can do."

Both Adam Wheatcroft and Ashley Kamuf did just that in gusty, stiff-wind conditions … and both won their respective gold medals!

It is essential for archers to believe in themselves. Their confidence should be in their ability to shoot perfect form. An archer is in control of few things during an archery tournament. If you control your form and execute the shot the same way every time, then you will shoot the tightest group that you are capable of achieving. You cannot do any better than that. When the game is over and all of the scorecards are in, then you can find out how well you did in comparison to the other competitors. Most archers who are upset at the end of a competition are not upset because they didn't win. They are disappointed because they failed to shoot as well as they did in practice.

What goes through your mind when you are shooting your best in practice? What goes through you mind when you are having trouble in a tournament? At a competition, too often the thought process becomes overwhelmed with the significance of the shoot and the focus on a winning score. This way of thinking is completely different from what happens in a practice setting. The attitude change during a tournament often results in a variation of form and more scattered arrow groups.

Worrying about score, winning or what the competition is doing only creates anxiety and muscle tension. When this occurs, it is very difficult to repeatedly produce the same shot. You cannot control score or winning, but you *can* control perfect shot execution. If your mind and body work together to make the perfect shot, then you can duplicate that form. If you allow your thought process to dwell on the scorecard, then the bond between what you are thinking and what your body is doing will be broken, making it very difficult to duplicate the shot. The perfect shot is nothing more than the mind and body working together as a single unit to produce a fluid shot execution.

The reason we practice is twofold. First, we practice because we love to shoot. Second, we practice so we can duplicate our form on every shot. The better we become at reproducing the shot, the tighter the arrow groups will be. This is when we are performing at our best. Put your trust, confidence and concentration where it belongs. Believe in your ability to execute the shot with the same form - every time.

Seven Ways to Remain Focused

Picture yourself in a tournament setting with one target remaining in the competition. You and another person in your shooting group are tied for first. Your opponent steps up and scores an 8 on a shot at a long, difficult turkey target. Now it is your turn. What is going through your mind? Are you thinking that you need to capture a 10 to win? Are you thinking that you have to at least score an 8? Are you concluding that you cannot hit a 5 or you will lose? Entertaining any of these thoughts can be detrimental to your game. Instead, you need to be focused on shooting the best form that you are capable of producing. Mentally block out anything that interferes with the task facing you, which is perfect shot execution. Many things can interrupt an archer's concentration; and once this happens, the performance will suffer. Ways to combat the distractions and help you remain focused include the following:

1. Use pre-tournament preparation: Do not think of the upcoming tournament in terms of winning or having a fabulous score. Instead, keep your focus on making every shot with the best form that you can produce. As you replicate your shot again and again, mentally "see" yourself using this form in the tournament setting.

2. Relax: The whole key to being able to execute good form is staying relaxed. Regulate your breathing by taking deep, slow breaths. Constantly remind yourself to drop your shoulders and relax your muscles.

3. Think performance: You know you can shoot great form because you do it constantly in practice. All you need to do is execute the same shot that you have been practicing.

4. Do not be concerned with results: Do not put any emphasis on your score or the score of others. You can think about that after the tournament is over. Dwelling on points while competing will distract you from a top performance.

5. Be totally involved in the moment: Forget the shots

that you have already taken and the ones that you are going to face. Only be concerned with the shot that is in front of you.

6. Do not give shots a more significant value: In the scenario at the beginning of this topic, most of you probably looked at the shot as a win or lose situation. With this attitude you placed a higher value on the arrow. Too often you will try to fine-tune your sight (over-aim) and then make a poor shot execution. This is just another arrow, so allow yourself to shoot the way you have practiced for months.

7. Use Mental Imagery: Before releasing the arrow, look at the target and visualize going through the motions of using perfect form. Let your body and mind feel the shot and then execute that same shot.

Distractions can easily interfere with your archery performance, so stay in the moment and concentrate on making each shot. If your mind wanders or detrimental thoughts creep in, stop what you are doing and refocus on executing your best form. Successful archers strive to develop self-discipline and a strong mental game.

Works Cited

Piper, Watty. *The Little Engine That Could.* New York: Platt and Munk Co. Inc., 1954. Print

Amberry, Tom. *Free Throw: 7 Ways to Success at the Free Throw Line*. New York: Harper Collins Publishers, 1996. Print.

ARCHERY: THINK AND SHOOT LIKE A CHAMPION